727.6971 CAR
Cardinal, Douglas, author.
Design principles : Canadian Museum of
History

DESIGN PRINCIPLES

CANADIAN MUSEUM OF HISTORY

Douglas Cardinal, Architect

This document was written by Douglas Cardinal with
input and assistance from colleagues in his architectural firm.

727.6
971
CAR

© Canadian Museum of History & Douglas Cardinal, 2016

All rights reserved. No part of this book may be reproduced or transmitted in any form or by any means, electronic or mechanical, including photocopying, recording or any retrieval system, without the prior written permission of the Canadian Museum of History. Every effort has been made to obtain permission for all copyright-protected work presented in this publication. If you have copyright-protected work in this publication and have not given permission, or to enquire about reproducing any section of this publication, please contact permissions@historymuseum.ca.

Library and Archives Canada Cataloguing in Publication
Cardinal, Douglas, author
Design principles: Canadian Museum of History /
Douglas Cardinal, architect.

Issued also in French under title:
Principes de conception : Musée Canadien de l'histoire.

ISBN 978-1-988282-04-6 (paperback)
Cat. No.: NM24-35/2016E

1. Cardinal, Douglas.
2. Canadian Museum of History – Design and construction.
3. Historical museums – Québec (Province) – Gatineau – Design and construction.
4. Museum architecture – Québec (Province) – Gatineau.
5. Gatineau (Québec) – Buildings, structures, etc.
I. Canadian Museum of History, issuing body.
II. Title.

NA6700.G38C37 2016
727'.6971009714221
C2016-906064-0

Published by the
Canadian Museum of History
100 Laurier Street
Gatineau, QC K1A 0M8
historymuseum.ca

Printed and bound in Canada.

CONTENTS

FOREWORD

ASSIGNMENT

INTRODUCTION

PART 1. THE VISION

Significant Features of the Site – Basic Shape and Forms – Major Functional Challenges – Seismic Design – Occupant Safety – A Typical Visitor Walkthrough – The Use of Computers in the 1980s – Fast-Tracking the Project With Multiple Contractors – What Inspired Me to Commit All Resources to the Project – From Vision to Reality: An Architect's Reflection on the Creation of the Museum

PART 2. DESIGN PRINCIPLES

Objectives – Design Philosophy – The Building as an Icon – The Building as Sculptural Form – Form and Function – Orientation and Relation – Plazas – Landscaping – Additive Architecture – Structural Expressions – Exhibits – Cross-Referencing – Technology – Light – Materials – Services

PART 3. THE FUTURE

Inspiration – Purpose – Technique – A Building as a Symbol – The Museum as Historical Art – Form and Function – Orientation and Flow – Setting and Meaning – Conclusion

FOREWORD

In 1982, the Government of Canada engaged in the design and construction of two iconic buildings in the heart of the capital to house and display the country's historical and cultural treasures. These new buildings were intended as legacy projects for all Canadians. The National Gallery of Canada was sited in Ottawa on Sussex Drive near the old War Museum and The National Museum of Man was to be located on the shores of the Ottawa River in Gatineau, Quebec, across from the Parliament buildings. The Canada Museums Construction Corporation was created to direct the design and construction of these two buildings, starting with a competition to select the most highly qualified Canadian architects to undertake these prestigious mandates.

Douglas Cardinal was selected from among twelve distinguished finalists as the architect of record for the National Museum of Man based on the strength of his vision. He stated to the competition judges that "The National Museum of Man grows out of the landscape and is indiscernible from it. It moves and flows with the contours of the land like a massive natural outcropping of stratified native rock in warm earth tones." Mr. Cardinal's consideration for visitors to feel the Museum's connection with nature and the grand curvilinear forms of its shapes while moving through its spaces has made an extraordinarily interesting experience that is truly Canadian.

Although the Museum has since changed names from the National Museum of Man to the Canadian Museum of Civilization in 1989 and then finally to the Canadian Museum of History in 2013, the architectural legacy created by Mr. Cardinal has persisted and evolved. Witness to this fact is that the Museum is the largest and most visited museum in the country, and the building is a must-see destination for tourists visiting the region. The Museum's formidable Grand Hall is the location of choice for most high level government functions and the view from the exterior plaza across the river to the Parliament buildings is one of the most sought after photographic opportunities in the region.

As President and Chief Executive Officer of the Canadian Museum of History, I proudly endorse this Legacy Document prepared by the Museum's principal design architect, Douglas Cardinal. This remarkable commentary on the design principles of the building will help the Museum meet the dual challenges of safeguarding Mr. Cardinal's vision and ensuring that any changes to the building continue to support its mandate and function.

It is my hope that this publication will serve as a model for other organizations and great Canadian architectural buildings, ensuring that generations to come are properly informed about the vision and guiding principles behind our country's distinguished architectural structures.

— Mark O'Neill
President and CEO
Canadian Museum of History

ASSIGNMENT

THE REQUEST TO THE ORIGINAL ARCHITECT

Inspired by a visit to Australia's Sydney Opera House, designed by Jørn Utzon, I approached Douglas Cardinal about producing a "Legacy Document of Design Principles" for the Canadian Museum of History. This document is to be a used as a permanent reference and guide for facility managers, exhibition designers, organizational leaders and other Museum stakeholders to ensure that the integrity of the original architect's vision is respected for posterity when contemplating or undertaking any future building modifications.

The document contains the principal design architect's original sketches, design drafts, photos and other visual aids to clearly illustrate the vision and design principles, complement the words of the text and help future users of this document understand Mr. Cardinal's design intent.

It is important for the reader to note that the Canadian Museum of History changed its name from the National Museum of Man in 1968 to the Canadian Museum of Civilization in 1989 and, finally, to its current name in 2013. These names appear in different parts of this document as they relate to the story of Douglas Cardinal's involvement as principal design architect of the Museum.

PART 1. THE VISION

For this document to be successful, it is important for future designers to understand what inspired the vision of the principal design architect. This section is intended to provide future designers with a starting point for studying the building and comprehending how the architect's original vision is expressed in the building's forms and functions. This understanding is fundamental to maintaining the integrity of the architect's original vision and allowing that vision to be carried through any contemplated design changes.

My first task, therefore, was to ask Mr. Cardinal to describe what inspired his vision for the building and how he addressed the opportunities and challenges offered by the site. I then asked him to explain how the design came about, what lead eventually to the design concept and the relationship of the building to its surroundings.

For the government of the time, the construction of new purpose-built buildings for the National Gallery of Canada and the National Museum of Man represented the most significant cultural legacy projects of the era. As a result, there was tremendous interest from stakeholders at all levels of government and within various government departments. This section is also where Mr. Cardinal describes the factors that influenced his vision for the Museum, his approach to design and construction and the effects these had on delivering the project.

PART 2. THE DESIGN PRINCIPLES

This section of the document is where the principal design architect establishes a clear set of principles for managing future design changes for the Canadian Museum of History. Mr. Cardinal's comments are made in the context of his understanding of the Canadian Museum of History's current and future needs.

This section is also where Mr. Cardinal presents the objectives and intent of the design principles and his views on why the building design matters. Fundamental design principles then may be presented in greater detail to guide future designers on environmental sustainability, building form, orientation, materiality, light, colour and other considerations.

Finally, the design principles contain Mr. Cardinal's recommendations on the planning approach for the process of maintaining the original vision.

PART 3. THE FUTURE

Naturally, a large, multifunction building such as the Canadian Museum of History will undergo many changes over time. As organizational needs change, there will be a need to modify the building to suit the operational functions and technologies of the day.

This section of the document describes how future changes to the building are to be undertaken to maintain the character of the original design. Therefore, it is important that Mr. Cardinal record the characteristics of the building that need to be respected to maintain important features such as the sightlines from outside and within the building, the general look and feel of the building's shapes and materials and the preservation of key architectural elements, without which the essence of the building's image could be irreparably harmed.

— Guy Larocque
Director, Facility Management
Canadian Museum of History

INTRODUCTION

The footprint prepared by Douglas Cardinal for the National Museum of Man on Parc Laurier in Hull is like two discs, two shells or, perhaps even more accurately, like two petals of a flower with a stamen. Its fluid, organic forms echo the structure of the site, accommodate — very efficiently — the needs of the Museum of Man, and declare that this is a work by the Alberta architect, Douglas Cardinal, working in tandem with the Montréal firm, Tétreault, Parent, Languedoc et Associés.

The new Museum of Man in its sheer originality should attract visitors to Hull. In fact, its sensuous forms could even seduce them there.

— Jean Sutherland Boggs
Chair, Canada Museum Construction Corporation
November 28, 1983

1

The greatest opportunity and professional accomplishment for an architect is to design a national building such as a museum that houses all the cultures of a nation. It is, for me, like designing a cathedral because it's an opportunity to develop in sculptural form an icon for the country — an icon that has an effect on every citizen. Prime Minister Pierre Trudeau told me that he wanted to develop symbols of a nation: a constitution to enshrine our rights, a national gallery to enshrine our arts and a national museum to enshrine our cultures. These are all symbols of nationhood, and I knew that designing a national symbol would be the highlight of my career.

When I was 18, I met Lawren Harris of the Group of Seven in Vancouver. He described to me his love of the powerful forms of nature that he abstractly painted, as well as the dramatic colours in our Canadian landscape. Inspired by natural forms, he used his classical training and ability as a painter to create a new style of art. This approach to developing art by observing and stylizing the natural environment of the Americas truly inspired me to evolve my own style of architecture.

People often ask me which architects or architecture influenced me to create my own signature style. When I studied architecture and the history of architecture in Texas, I was really inspired by the Baroque, the Renaissance and the later Art Nouveau period, where all the arts — painting, sculpture, architecture and music — came together. I studied the work of Baromini and the Italian masters, Michelangelo and Bernini, as well as later architects such as Alvar Aalto, Antoni Gaudí, Bruce Goff, Charles Rennie Mackintosh, Louis Sullivan and particularly Frank Lloyd Wright. In terms of philosophy, spirituality and organic form, I felt more akin to Rudolph Steiner, who created the Waldorf schools. I developed my whole philosophy and approach to architecture from my education and my work in Texas. It was an enlightening, historic time. The human rights movement was raising social consciousness. This humanistic training culminated in my first major work: St. Mary's Church in Red Deer, Alberta. I wanted to develop a truly signature style of architecture that was a unique expression of a free individual in a free society. I did not want to conform to any other academic style. My colleagues defined my work as classically organic, and the Friends of Kebyar of the Frank Lloyd Wright school of thought have adopted my work as part of their philosophy. I believe that organic architecture helps us create balance and harmony between the environment and ourselves.

1. THE VISION

The Canadian Museum of History is a sculptural form that grows out of the landscape and is indiscernible from it. The sculptural form moves and flows with the contours of the land similar to a massive natural outcropping of stratified, native rock in warm earth tones. The surrounding natural settings of Laurier Park, Jacques Cartier Park and the Ottawa River seem to flow into the building as flourishing plants and cascading water, while the earth itself wraps around and over the building like a green mantle. The inner life of the Museum — the throngs of people — flow out onto the riverside park, outdoor exhibits, sunlit plazas and an open-air theatre. The architectural forms bend and curve, encouraging people to traverse the terraces of the building. While moving through these terraces, visitors experience a series of exciting architectural moments such as skylights, crystalline pools, stone-sheathed forms of mechanical shafts that project through the roof, open-air exhibits, unique sculptures, plants and the natural landscape surrounding Parliament Hill. These terraces also include a pedestrian concourse that links the south landing of the site with the marina at the north end.

SIGNIFICANT FEATURES OF THE SITE

Douglas Cardinal, who has always had a deep sense of harmony with nature, has been given a site that would arouse the poet in any architect, but particularly in one who is an author as well (Of the Spirit, 1977). Laurier Park is a low sloping site by the Ottawa River used as an encampment by Indians and explorers in the 18th and 19th centuries, and it has picturesque views, not just of the Victorian Gothic Parliament Buildings but also of the cascading terminal locks of the old Rideau Canal.

To the north, the Alexandra (or Interprovincial) Bridge links the site with Ottawa. The main approach, however, is from Laurier Street in Hull, which the new building will animate with its theatres, its café, a museum shop and its welcoming entrances and dramatic esplanade. On the southwest of the site will be a direct link with the Maison du Citoyen, a city hall and community centre with extensive underground parking. It is even possible that there will one day be a campus of the University of Quebec to the west across Laurier.

In designing for the site, Cardinal had to give an urban presence on Laurier Street while providing views across the river both from the intersection of Laurier and Boulevard des Allumettières, northwest of the site and through the building by fanning it open midway along its facade to create the entrance esplanade. The forms of the riverfront open up like a flower. Since the Museum will be seen often from the heights — the escarpment of Parliament, the Interprovincial Bridge, Nepean Point with the new National Gallery and office buildings in Hull and Ottawa — Cardinal has made of the roofscape a harmonious but varied combination of forms.

— Canadian Museum Construction Corporation
Ottawa Document
1983

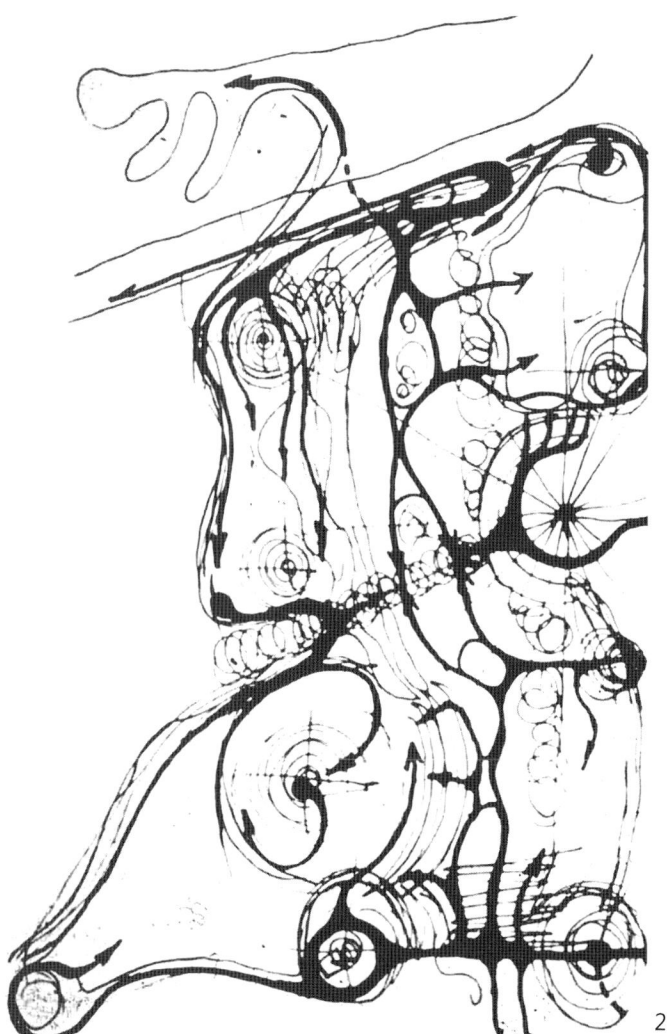

BASIC SHAPE AND FORMS

The building rises up in the form of gentle terraces three stories above Confederation Boulevard (Laurier Street). It then cascades downward, transforming into broad, sweeping terraces to the flood-line at the riverside. It thus offers a low, modest profile toward the urban setting of Gatineau, while presenting a majestic view from across the river in appropriate scale with the sweeping lines of the riverbank.

The building cuts into the slopes of the riverbank so large areas on the urban side requiring a stable environment, a high degree of security or rigid controls on lighting may be buried in the ground, allowing the desired levels of controls with a minimum of imposed barriers. The stepped façade towards the river, on the other hand, is open and inviting; it is enclosed and shielded from the snow-bearing winds by a sloping, faceted glass wall that shimmers like a jewel in the morning sun and radiates like a lighted crystal by night. Inside is a vibrant year-round park, a haven for those who endure our long winters.

The Museum is positioned to respect the existing pedestrian route diagonally across Laurier Park toward the marina. The building's main axis is aligned with the Parliament Buildings, so that the Grand Hall always highlights this dramatic view. The building is pulled out toward the river to the edge of the rock shelf, where it both commands a better view up and down the river and is seen by people arriving by boat.

MAJOR FUNCTIONAL CHALLENGES

The requirements for the Museum were similar to the requirements for a hospital operating room. To protect the artifacts, the mechanical engineering was designed by working closely with the international engineering company Cosentini Associates, whose head office is located in New York City. The mechanical system is geothermal, sustainably using the water from the Ottawa River to heat and cool the building.

All the spaces were designed to be digitally controlled so the humidity and temperature matched the exact specifications of the Canadian Conservation Institute and the National Research Council of Canada. To accomplish this, we created computer programs to run the whole complex. Sensors were placed in individual spaces that were designed to monitor the movement and effects of large crowds, which add temperature and humidity to the spaces. By monitoring the environment, the building retains the same temperature and humidity no matter what changes may occur.

5

SEISMIC DESIGN

The Museum site is located in a major earthquake zone. To design an organic structure in such a zone meant that two members from the appointed structural engineering team had to work with me directly in my Edmonton office. They were very creative about developing a structure that would accommodate my curvilinear organic forms while also meeting the special requirements of the site. The Museum complex is essentially divided into 12 separate buildings with expansion joints to resolve the challenges of earthquake design, and the structure is a combination of reinforced concrete and structural steel. We had to provide all the dimensions for the structural steel fabricator, as well as the exact dimensions for all of the base plates in the concrete. We provided these exact dimensions so the curvilinear trusses would be built accurately and constructed so that all the curves would come together perfectly. Accomplishing this required flawless coordination of the architectural and structural teams from my office, with the aid of our computers.

OCCUPANT SAFETY

Cross-referencing was a major vision of the Museum staff; however, it required interconnected floor spaces, which posed a problem with the existing fire safety regulations and the environmental conditions in each hall. Particularly challenging were the systems for venting smoke and evacuating the public to protect them from fire or smoke inhalation. Code consultants worked with us to create a system that would help protect the public even better than the existing codes and still have the interconnected floor spaces.

Interconnected openings have air curtains to control the temperature within each hall. There is also an appropriately designed smoke exhaust system. In case of a fire, there is a delayed reaction before the sprinklers engage to allow enough time to use local fire extinguishers, because water can damage the artifacts as much as fire and smoke. With the sprinklers and smoke exhaust system, people have means of egress in each hall that will take them directly to the outside of the building with proper fire escapes. In the design of all exhibits, protecting the public and protecting the environmental conditions must be respected by the exhibit designers.

A TYPICAL VISITOR WALKTHROUGH[1]

The former Museum of Man, now the Canadian Museum of History, opened in 1989 with the name Canadian Museum of Civilization. A puzzling name at the time, the Museum promised to be a showcase of all the cultures that made the wondrous fabric that is Canadian society. I had already seen the impressive historical and ethnographic collections, and I knew that the new Museum would be perfect for showcasing and cherishing all the precious artifacts that reflected Canada's development as a nation. It was decided that the lower floor along the Grand Hall would be dedicated the Aboriginal Peoples of Canada. The upper floor, the Canada Hall, became a walk through time and space of this great country of ours, and was dedicated largely to the story of the emigrant nations. The middle floor was dedicated to showcasing temporary exhibits created from in-house initiatives and international museum lenders.

The program and design of the Museum was thus complex and ambitious, as it was to house much of the historical and ethnographical treasures of the country. Since it was created with a radical change in mind, everybody involved understood there would be many more changes in the future.

The building and exhibit technologies therefore needed to be designed and constructed with flexibility in mind. It was clear that the specifics of showcasing these treasures would change as time passed and Canadian society evolved. Technologies change, social values and understandings change, and the building itself needed to be designed to embrace the change that organically occurs in society. Within the stability of form, like the embodiment of the country itself, the building can evolve by respecting the organic principles of its inception. Indeed, the organic forms and technical systems of the building allow and encourage dynamic change in the future.

The Outside — The Plazas

As visitors cross the Alexandra Bridge, the massive yet sinuous building of the Canadian Museum of History appears to be alive — both enticing and unique. As they step onto the plaza, the scale of the architecture changes: the building becomes very personal, warm and nurturing.

6

[1.] *This section was written by Idoia Arana-Beobide de Cardinal, Managing Director, Douglas Cardinal Architect, Inc. and former Canadian Museum of History tour guide.*

Centered, visitors look at Parliament Hill, which surely represents the heart of the country. It is then when visitors realize that the two buildings feel like open arms to receive them on a cultural adventure. Visitors understand that, symbolically and physically, they are indeed embraced by Canadian culture. The water that was to be in the plaza is still missing, but the senses urge the visitors to walk forward to the sparkling sound of the water of the reflecting pool. There, the water cascades along the magnificent staircases guiding visitors to the lower plaza, which acts as a stage while the stairs themselves can be used for sitting, as in an amphitheatre. The landscape and view to the Ottawa River, Parliament Hill and all other national buildings is simply spectacular.

Realizing they are surrounded by the best of Canada and its culture, visitors look at the two distinctive buildings: the Curatorial Building and the Museum Building.

Curatorial Building

On the left is the curatorial wing, which is where all of Canada's most precious artifacts are stored — deep in the middle of the building, physically and psychologically protected by the Museum staff, whose offices run along the periphery of the building. This has advantages. First, the artifacts themselves, the most precious contents of the Museum, are perfectly buffered from the outside. Second, having all offices in the periphery of the building allows the employees to enjoy windows and natural light. On the top floor, the office of the director has a spectacular view of Parliament Hill and the Ottawa River — the perfect scenery for nation-building and inspiring meetings.

Museum Main Lobby

Still facing Parliament Hill, to the right is the entrance to the public display wing of the Museum. This building relies on male forms as vertical elements, and bolder forms express the vigorous manifestation of cultural expressions. The entrance — a totem-like head — represents the guardian of that which is shown and celebrated; the symbolic mind of the organism that is the Museum itself. As visitors enter the Museum through the figurative guardian head structure, they may feel that they will consciously comprehend, celebrate and understand the many cultural expressions inside. A sculpture on the ceiling of the entrance vestibule representing the Northern Lights reminds visitors somehow of the interconnectedness of nature and social human evolution. The art in the building becomes intrinsic to the blending of architecture and Museum programming — a blending that is powerful and attracts visitors into the lobby.

The exhibit wing is divided into four floors, each with a distinctive type of exhibit. In the main floor lobby, visitors quickly realize that there is a three-way fork: to the right, they find the Canadian Children's Museum and the theatres; in the middle are the Special Exhibitions Galleries; and to the left, the amazing view into the Grand Hall, which introduces us to the Aboriginal Peoples exhibits on the lower level.

Canadian Children's Museum

The Canadian Children's Museum is a rhapsody of colours, sounds and experiences. In a childlike fantasy world, architectural settings illustrate life in different locations of the world. Children carry a passport that they can have stamped at all these locations. They can dress up according to the culture and engage in an activity typical of the area, be it a Pakistani bus, a Mexican market, a Japanese house or the pyramid of Egypt. The extension of the Museum outside shows the intricate relationship of the exhibits, the architecture and the landscape to allow the Museum to effortlessly run all the different programs.

The Theatres

Next to the Children's Museum is the CINÉ+ (formerly IMAX®) movie theatre, a dark blue wonder holding both a huge, seven-storey high screen and a dome screen with 180° field of vision. The original IMAX® Theatre was the first in the world to combine both IMAX® (the screen) and OMNIMAX® (the dome) technologies in a single location. The extraordinary engineering that allowed for this achievement was also an intricate part of the design of the Museum. One can inherently appreciate the harmony of form and function blended in this space. The feeling of wonder, excitement and eager discovery of the films is carried into the very space enclosing the visitors.

A very different feeling, but equally emotional, is the space of the Theatre. The flowing curves and red colour scheme are reminiscent of the golden era of Victorian theatres. It also reflects the modernist organic expression of the essence of the many great theaters and opera houses of Europe. During social occasions, pedestrians on Laurier Street can witness the mingling of theatre patrons in the Marius Barbeau Lobby through the large windows exposed to the street. The same large windows that run the extension of the wall end at the Museum's coffee shop and bistro (a space previously taken by the gift shop). The existing setup is mindful of the original design intent: engage pedestrians through retail inside the Museum so they might experience its unique cultural offerings.

Special Exhibition Galleries

Back at the lobby, visitors can also take the straight route to the Special Exhibition Galleries. These large areas provide rigorous standards for environmental control in order to display both travelling exhibits from the great museums of the world and theme exhibits created by the Museum itself. The Special Exhibitions Corridor is framed by a large window that, through a screen, allows visitors to perceive the Grand Hall below.

This idea of cross-referencing the exhibition spaces was the unique vision of the Museum's past Director General, George MacDonald. He wanted visitors to clearly visualize the volume and space of the Museum, as well as be enticed to continue their visit. Many world museums feature maze-like, tightly controlled exhibit paths with no relation to the museum's own architecture. The Canadian Museum of History is unique in that architecture and exhibits were designed to work together. The architects worked closely with Museum code representatives to protect the public from any danger presented by the open spaces of the balconies. The engineering required for creating the strict humidity and climatologically balanced environment for the safe-keeping of the exhibits in these open spaces was an achievement in itself.

From Canada Hall to Canadian History Hall

The staircase at the end of the Grand Hall, now gloriously illuminated by Alex Janvier's *Morning Star*, can take us either downstairs to the River View Salon and the Aboriginal exhibits or upstairs to what was once the entrance to the Canada Hall. When it opened in 1989, Canada Hall presented in life-sized dioramas the lives and experiences of emigrants from different nations as they came, settled and built Canada, in the East from the Viking settlement of L'Anse aux Meadows in 1200 to the West Coast in the 19th century and the Yukon explorations in the 1960s.

This elaborate exhibition gave historical and architectural context to selected great moments in Canada. But the linear narrative was limited to the arrival of the emigrant settlers and did not truly reflect the history of Canada. Also, its maze-like structure overpowered the original intent of the architectural space to show the expanse of Canada and its cross-referenced connectedness.

Occupying the same space as that of the Canada Hall, the architectural design of the new Canadian History Hall is intended to reflect the magnificence of the grand, open spaces of Canada. The tall curved ceiling that symbolizes the sky itself bends with the mezzanine level, following the sinuousness of the Hall. In the middle, a grand staircase reminiscent of Asticou (the "Great Kettle" of Chaudière Falls in the heart of the nation's capital) becomes the Hall's hub.

Opening on July 1, 2017, the new Canadian History Hall will explain the history of Canada from the last Ice Age with the arrival of Aboriginal Peoples. This holistic understanding of history, ethnology, archeology and anthropology, along with historical disciplines and artifacts, will demonstrate the rich history of Canada. The new gallery will reflect the complex multidisciplinary and multifaceted history of Canada. In this organic approach to history, objects and events will be expressed by different voices to recognize the different aspects and experiences of the people who built and developed Canada as a nation.

Grand Hall

Looking down from the David M. Stewart Salon (at what was once the exit to the Canada Hall, and will become the entrance to the new Canadian History Hall), the visitor sees a life-sized diorama representing a typical Aboriginal West Coast village. Once there, the visitor realizes the vastness of the space, an area as large as a football field. The sculpted columns inside and outside are stylized representations of the peoples of all cultures coming together in the Grand Hall.

7

Proud and elongated — some taller, some smaller — we are all in essence the same, celebrating and sharing each other's contributions to the planet.

Rich in symbolism and fluid in its interpretation, the columns also represent inverted oars as visitors walk along the window. The oars vigorously paddle the canoe-like hull that is the ceiling of the Grand Hall. Visitors feel like they are inside a vessel, taking them on an adventure.

The large windows are another architectural wonder, integrating sophisticated engineering to conserve the right environmental settings — humidity, light and temperature — through the whole space. All the windows have diffusers that blow air onto them, similar to the defrosting system in cars.

The Grand Hall is simply magnificent. This is the reason why it has been used as the stage and backdrop for many private and official receptions for world heads of state. The opulent galas have a unique Canadian backdrop as the Aboriginal culture of the West Coast fascinates all who witness it. The West Coast village diorama illustrates six different cultures of the West Coast, stylized as they would be in their natural settings. The technical and architectural integration of this complex exhibit environment include the representation of the forest, seashore, rocks and water one should expect on the West Coast. The houses themselves exhibit different aspects of the Pacific Coast First Nations, and were designed and erected in location by the Aboriginal Peoples they represent.

As an Anishinabe, Douglas Cardinal was included in the ceremonies for the blessing of the dwellings. Thus the Grand Hall achieved a very unique and special technical, artistic and spiritual integration with the architect and its architecture. The old totem poles are proudly and properly displayed, and all who enter the Grand Hall irrevocably feel a reverence toward Aboriginal cultures.

The Grand Hall also includes an exhibition space showing a reproduction of archaeological excavations carried out from 1966 to 1978 in the Prince Rupert region on the West Coast. In the setting of an ancient forest, this exhibition presents both archaeological and ethnological elements, teaching visitors about the way of life of the Tsimshian nation, the role of the archaeologist and the need to understand archaeology and Indigenous cultures.

First Peoples Hall

The First Peoples Hall celebrates the history, diversity, creativity, resourcefulness and endurance of Canada's First Nations, Métis and Inuit peoples. In doing so, it presents a vivid record of cultural richness and a story of survival, renewal and vitality.

Through more than 2,000 historical and contemporary objects, images and documents presented in fairly standard museological fashion, the First Peoples Hall depicts the traditional cultures of Aboriginal Peoples across Canada and how European contact and settlement impacted the people and their cultures. Visitors will encounter ceremonial and everyday objects, such as clothing and tools, as well as some of the oldest artifacts in the Museum's collection — amongst them one of the oldest representations of a human face. Visitors will also discover ancient and contemporary interpretations of myths and other traditional ways of knowledge, as well as videos, art and vivid dioramas. They will learn about the achievements of contemporary Aboriginal Peoples in every aspect of Canadian society — as artists, athletes, writers, soldiers, teachers, political leaders and more.

In between the Pacific Coast exhibits and the First Peoples Hall there is a large space occasionally used as a Special Exhibition Gallery. Flanked by the Northern and Southern Salons, these elegant gathering spaces host functions and receptions of all kinds.

Cafeteria and Other Spaces

From the W. E. Taylor Salon at the base of the escalators, and heading away from the Grand Hall, visitors encounter the newly dedicated Douglas Cardinal Salon and the Resource Centre. Walking along this hallway, visitors can see the Parliament Buildings beautifully framed by the waterfall of the staircase outside. At the end of the hallway, the Voyageurs Cafeteria is equally shared by Museum staff and visitors seeking nourishment and rest while they enjoy the spectacular views of the Ottawa River, Parliament Hill and all other major government buildings. Canada here blends the beauty of its natural setting with the wonderful architectural statements that create its national identity. Canada, here, is magnificent.

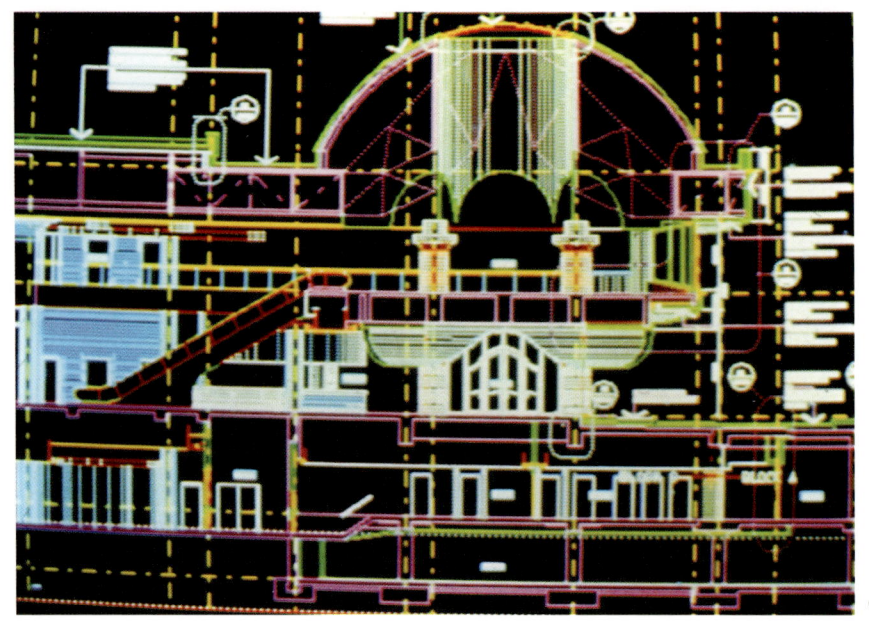

9

THE USE OF COMPUTERS IN THE 1980s

The knowledge of computers and the computer technology we developed during our work on the Museum was invaluable for completing the demands of the project. Owing to the organic nature of the project, we had to provide all the contractors, subcontractors, material suppliers and trades with the dimensions of all the components and systems. We developed a computer model with 15 decimal place accuracy so we could describe the coordinates for every curve, every elevation and every layout throughout the project. We were, at that time, the only fully computerized architectural company using computer-aided design (CAD) programs for all aspects of architecture. To design and build our organic building efficiently, we created our own Linux-based computer software in 1978. The Museum was the 13th building we designed and managed solely by computer technology.

Our technology was so advanced that the federal government needed to provide our Montréal partners with matching computers so we could collaboratively run our unique software. This was, of course, before any architectural software was widely implemented. We provided our partners, Tétreault, Parent, Languedoc et Associés (TPL), with the database so our drawings would be compatible. We were in charge of producing all the structural drawings on the computer and supplied the contractors with exact dimensions to coordinate with the structure. We also created interference drawings for the mechanical and electrical systems to be integrated with the structural and architectural drawings. The computer capacity of our team and our Montréal partners was essential to carry out the mandate of the Prime Minister and the Canada Museum Construction Corporation.

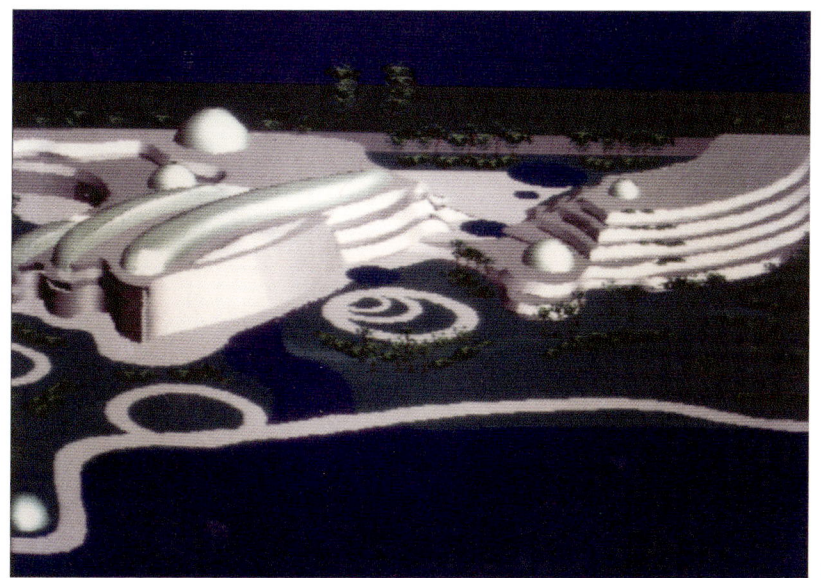

10

11

Dear Mr. Cardinal:

Let me express my sincere appreciation for the very interesting and informative talk and demonstration that you gave me and my officials regarding your use of computer-aided design technology. I was particularly impressed with the obviously very effective use to which you are putting this exciting new technology in your architectural practice.

Clearly CAD has enabled you to increase the level of accuracy and detail in your design, while removing much of the tediousness and monotony involved in preparing working drawings. More importantly, I can see now where it has enabled you to undertake designs of a complexity and sophistication that would not have been possible using more traditional approaches.

Yours truly,

J. A. H. Mackay
Deputy Minister, Department of Public Works
December 30, 1983

12

FAST-TRACKING THE PROJECT WITH MULTIPLE CONTRACTORS

I had to develop some 265 separate contracts and a process of sequential tendering with the construction manager, Concordia Construction Inc. Each of the 265 documents we had to produce became an even greater task because each package produced tender documents. After tendering and selecting a contractor, we performed value engineering to reduce the cost to a minimum, with input from the contractor, and therefore our documents had to be modified for construction documents. When the contractors were finished marking up these documents after their part of the construction, we had to develop another set of as-built drawings so the next contractor in sequence would have the precise data to build upon.

13

Canadian Museum of Civilization – Facing South from Place du Portage (May 2, 1984)

Canadian Museum of Civilization – Facing South from Place du Portage (April 29, 1985)

WHAT INSPIRED ME TO COMMIT ALL RESOURCES TO THE PROJECT

It took eight months to get the approval of 15 government departments and the National Capital Commission to move forward. The following day, the Prime Minister and I met so he would be fully acquainted with every aspect of the design in detail. He presented it to Cabinet, obtained their approval and the very next day directed me to start construction. The project was still in the schematics stage of design. We therefore had to redesign all the systems following the architectural concepts and sequential tendering during all phases of construction. In essence, we were designing and building at the same time to meet my commitment to the Government of Canada and to the Canada Museum Construction Corporation.

After the government changed in 1984, I decided that the best way to serve the project and the vision entrusted for all Canadians was to move to Ottawa. I found it necessary since the whole project needed to be fast-tracked.

I moved my office into the same building as the Canada Museum Construction Corporation and our architectural partners, Tétreault, Parent, Languedoc et Associés (TPL) in order to serve them every hour, since communication was so vital in orchestrating some 265 contracts within the corporation schedules and budgets. We also had to support the construction managers and contractors onsite, as well as our partners, TPL, onsite and in Montréal. Our meetings were shared by the Canada Museums Construction Corporation and were expedited because of our proximity.

FROM VISION TO REALITY:
AN ARCHITECT'S REFLECTION ON THE CREATION OF THE MUSEUM[2]

[2] *This section was written by Satish Rao, Senior Architect at Douglas Cardinal Architect, Inc.*

"The most significant building built in Canada after the Parliament Buildings."

"The sanctity of a temple, the complexity of an intensive care unit..."

"...the joy of celebration..."

"...a monument to a man's achievement..."

These are some of the words used by the public and the press to describe the Canadian Museum of Civilization (now Canadian Museum of History) project. From the extensive media coverage this building has received, there can be little doubt in anyone's mind that the Museum is a complex undertaking and a monumental challenge to all those who participated in bringing it to reality.

One challenge that such a project poses to the architect may be readily identified: resolving exacting technical problems. Demanding though this may be, addressing technical issues can be handled satisfactorily through diligent research, the use of available technology and a technically strong team.

But the Museum is far more than just a technical challenge: it is envisioned to be the very symbol of Canada as a nation, a monument to the achievement of its peoples and a symbol of the nation's promise for the future. It embodies the heritage, the culture and the very fabric and identity of the nation, both in its interior and exterior form, itself an artifact of our times. It sets a new standard for museums around the world.

To bring this national dream to reality in a way that speaks to the highest ideals of the country takes much more than technical competence; it takes a whole new way of thinking, indeed a whole different way of being.

This section, therefore, is not about what it takes to design a technically correct building or the clever solutions and devices we used during design and construction. This section is about the leadership and the particular way of being that was required to steer this project through the vast sea of technical, political and logistical hurdles to a successful conclusion, and the personal and organizational transformations that were necessary before the project could be realized.

This is not to say that the project did not have stringent technical requirements. In 1983, the Canada Museums Construction Corporation handed us a four-volume program of requirements — each volume approximately the size of a New York City telephone book — compiled by the National Museum of Man staff in conjunction with the National Museums Corporation. Although this document embodied over four years of work by a special task force and set down the requirements for each of the building's 500 rooms under some 80 headings that dealt with the quantitative aspects, it was not a suitable basis for design purposes. We had to supplement it with another two volumes of similar size, for the most part determining and recording requirements of a qualitative nature; that is, the type of atmosphere, character or ambience desired for each room. This process extended well into the design stages as each successive design presentation we made revealed a fresh aspect of the functions and their needs.

Put in very simple terms, the Museum consists essentially of two components. One is the public areas, containing those spaces where visitors will normally be permitted, such as the exhibit halls and galleries, the lobbies, the Grand Hall, the auditorium, the CINÉ+ movie theatre, the restaurant, the cafeteria and so on. The other is the curatorial areas, where visitors will not normally be admitted, consisting of administrative offices, the collections holding areas, the curatorial offices, laboratories, workshops and so on.

Both components had to be designed to the stringent and unforgiving requirements needed to protect and conserve a huge collection of invaluable artifacts. In addition, components also had to be designed for the safety and protection of the visiting public. Each type of artifact, depending on the materials from which it was made, required different humidity and temperature conditions that had to remain constant at all times. Few artifacts could tolerate the ultraviolet content of natural sunlight without experiencing rapid colour fading and organic deterioration. The most precious and sensitive artifacts had to be housed in chambers following the "onion-skin" principle: rooms arranged in five successive layers of security, with the security level increasing in each inner layer.

The building also housed a communications and data network consisting of over 30 systems serving such diverse functions as inventory controls, building security, data base storage and retrieval, video teleconferencing and a host of others.

In addition to these and other technical considerations too numerous to name, there were the logistical problems of managing a vast team of professionals, specialists and advisors. Although we were chosen from among 80 architects in a nation-wide search, we were required to associate with an architectural firm from Quebec since the project was being built in that province. This meant coordinating our work with TPL. Then there were the structural, mechanical and electrical engineers, and other consultants in such specialty areas such as lighting, landscaping, security, theatre and acoustics, totalling some 30 consultants and sub-consultants.

Most of these were from the Province of Quebec. Bilingualism, therefore, obviously became a significant element in the management of this project, and all of the 15,000 drawings had to be notated in both English and French. Right at the outset of the project, it was agreed that all documents and correspondence originating in Quebec would be prepared in French and all those originating in our office would be in English, with the recipient responsible for translation. Before long, our office was functionally bilingual.

In addition to the professionals, we were also required to coordinate input from some 50 different government departments, branches or agencies with such varied roles and specialties as the National Research Council's involvement with testing windows or the air quality guidelines of the Department of the Environment. Each member of this army of professionals and bureaucrats was obviously either an accomplished individual with a proven command over his or her respective field or a civil servant whose job responsibility placed him or her in a specific function role on the Museum team. To each and every one of them, the Museum probably represented the most significant — and in some cases also the largest — project of her or his career and therefore the success of the project, and especially the effectiveness of his or her contribution to it, could be expected to have a significant impact on his or her future. The stakes were therefore high and the deep intensity with which each individual participated in the project was not surprising. Each person would defend his or her recommendations or designs vigorously, and it was our responsibility, as architects, to coordinate diverse input from all these angles into a harmonious overall design, much like the conductor of a symphony orchestra.

Then there were the factors imposed by the decision to adopt the fast-tracking method for the project, whereby the construction of portions of the project is allowed to get underway while designs and drawings are still being prepared for other portions.

Such a method (often used for large projects, particularly in the private sector) offers several advantages. With this method, rather than waiting until drawings are completed — which, for a project of this size, could take over three years — certain trades can be tendered as soon as drawings are ready for them. This captures the market prices of the date and, if unaffected by the inevitable price escalation of the subsequent months, results in cost savings. The process was also expected to allow some flexibility in budgetary controls because, as each new trade is tendered, a fresh opportunity becomes available to review overall costs, and adjustments to the budget, design, materials and so on can be made. With fast-tracking, the design can also be current; that is, the architect can, at each decision-making point in the project, choose the best option, materials or system available at the time — the state-of-the-art, as it were — rather than be bound by only those choices that were available when the drawings were first completed.

One of the more significant benefits of fast-tracking, in this case, was the Canadian government's desire to get the project underway in the shortest time possible. The government of the day was anxious to have the project rise out of the ground and quickly become visible to the public.

Notwithstanding these advantages of fast-tracking, the process also imposes great hardship on the architect and consultants. The architect, in effect, is forced to finalize the design for portions of the building and authorize construction before there is an opportunity to fully resolve the overall design, which is a crucial part of the back-and-forth process of architectural design. Each successive portion that is built thus becomes a constraint in the design of all those elements that will be built after it.

Also, because the production of designs and drawings in the architect's office is closely related to construction work proceeding on the site, there is massive pressure on the entire design team to keep up with construction and demands for information, drawings and clarifications from the jobsite. In addition to these logistical problems with fast-tracking, there is also always the risk of a change in government, with the accompanying threat of a change in direction for the project when portions of it are already built.

Owing to these inherent problems with the process, the project must be expected to suffer from a certain number of so-called bad decisions that could in some cases result in the demolition and rebuilding of elements already erected. Therefore, when a government chooses the fast-tracking route it must, when allocating funds and establishing schedules, allow for such mishaps.

Aware of all these ramifications, we nevertheless went along with the fast-tracking method, accepting it as a reality of the project and committing ourselves to producing the best results possible within this system.

The last of the major considerations for the project were its several political ramifications. The political impact of a project of the nature and size of a national museum can hardly be overstated. The project was launched by the government led by Pierre Trudeau and soon became a symbol of the country's achievements and aspirations — a shrine for the safe-keeping of the nation's treasures. The site chosen for the building — directly across the river from the Parliament Buildings and on a premium spot along Confederation Boulevard — bore testimony to the perceived importance of this building. We were constantly aware that the progress of the building and its design, costs and schedules — in fact, anything that had to do with this project — was significant and attracted considerable political, media and public attention.

Owing to its location, the building came under the jurisdiction of the National Capital Commission. As a result, we were required to comply with several guidelines that governed its positioning on the site and its relationships to the several historic views and vistas across the river toward Parliament Hill. In addition to these guidelines, even the overall design of the building and the treatment of the surrounding grounds were required to meet with the approval of the Design Advisory Panel of the National Capital Commission, a panel made up of distinguished architects and landscape architects from across the country. We made innumerable presentations to this group before securing their full approval and endorsement of the design.

Funds available for the sister projects, the National Museum of Man (now Canadian Museum of History) and the National Art Gallery, were equally divided between the two, although the Museum was a much larger building on a considerably larger site. These funds were based on the initial program of space requirements, which was approximately 560,000 square feet. The supplementary programming process we undertook soon revealed that the space actually required to accommodate all the planned activities, facilities and building systems for the Museum amounted to almost a million square feet. For much of the design process, we were designing a $160 million building with an $80 million budget. This meant that the project was being designed with unrealistic, in fact impossible, budget constraints, and we put forward several recommendations that were turned down or diluted for reasons based on the old budget.

Added to all of this was the constant involvement — sometimes constructive, sometimes critical and questioning — of a number of bodies ranging from the Canada Museums Construction Corporation and the Department of Public Works to the media and the public, all functioning like ever-present watchdogs to this milestone event happening across from Parliament Hill. To the architect, it was like conducting his most important symphony with a vast orchestra of musicians while composing the music at the same time — all the while plugged into earphones through which the critics were handing down their reviews and admonitions!

These were the challenges we faced in designing what is now known as the Canadian Museum of History. By the standards of any normal architectural project, there was enough justification in these problems for a sound case of throwing in the towel.

To merely survive on the project, to merely produce the required number of drawings at the required times and in the required manner, took an incredible toll on our design team. In addition to the work carried out in about a dozen other offices simultaneously, the 20-member staff of our own office worked 15 to 17 hour days for three years to satisfy the needs of contractors hungry for information and civil servants hungry for explanations and reasons. To respond even more rapidly to the needs of the project, our team even relocated from Edmonton to Ottawa, suffering personal hardships and monetary losses.

We had to function as architects in the milieu of bureaucratic committees and meetings, providing reasons for every decision, engaging in debates and studies, and developing options for even the most instinctive and artistic choices. We had to incessantly buck questions and challenges from a vast empire of officials. It became evident right from the start of the project that we would be spending a smaller share of our energies and talents in the actual design than attending meetings and writing reports.

As a servant of the government, we had to respect the wishes of our client. Yet as the architect for the project, we knew that, once the project was complete, the sole legal and professional responsibility for each and every decision, each error, each judgement or misjudgement — literally for each stroke of the pen and each stone in the building — would rest with us. We therefore had to approach each decision as if our lives depended on it.

We have often been asked: how did we drive through all of this to produce the final results? How did we retain a clear picture of our vision and the vision of the government for this national symbol? What does it take to persist in the original goal in the face of impossibility? What does it take to bring about consensus among a vast number of people and agencies, each with a different, sometimes totally opposing, interpretation of the same goal, even in the face of lack of payment? In short, what does it take to achieve something of excellence and integrity?

We found that the normal measure of dedication and technical know-how was not enough. We learned what it really takes. The learning gradually transformed our office to, in the words of Andrew Nikiforuk of *Equinox Magazine*, "a cross between a boot camp and a monastery."

It takes a total commitment, a commitment to complete, no matter what; not just a commitment to trying hard, but a total commitment to a specific set of results. There were many times when the odds seemed insurmountable, the exercise totally futile; when it appeared that we stood alone in our commitment to achieve something more than the usual for this project and for the country. At such times, we had to read and re-read the big words we had plastered on the walls of our office, reminding us of our commitment to a specific set of results.

Then it takes a total sacrifice, a total disengagement from personal considerations. There were many times when, seeing the relatively peaceful and unthreatened lives that our friends and colleagues were living, we wondered why we should continue to push and struggle so. For years our personal lives, our families and our finances had all taken a dismal second place to the dictates and demands of this one project. The temptation was incredibly, excruciatingly persuasive to say, "I must sell the presentation short,

I haven't slept in three days," or "I'll have to pass up this problem, my slate is already full," or "I can't admit my error, I'll look like a fool." But we knew that if anything was to be achieved on this project — or in any worthwhile endeavour, for that matter — we could not afford to succumb to such considerations or listen to those who would persuade us to do so.

Then it takes communication; the power and ability to transmit this commitment to the other professionals and bureaucrats on the project, to empower them to take on the same commitment, to inspire them to make the vision their own, to align everyone on the team to a common goal. We found that, when our own single-minded dedication showed through, a similar commitment would develop all around us, sometimes in the most unlikely places, and things would suddenly, magically, fall into place. We found that there is an incredible power in empowering others to single-minded commitment.

Then it takes trust, the willingness to acknowledge that others on the team are committed to the same goals; that they all wish and strive for the very best for the project. It takes a willingness to give up our grip on the project in order to let others share in its leadership. We found that things worked best when we entrusted major roles and responsibilities to others, and then acknowledged their contribution in those roles.

In short, it takes a whole different way of being. Our every act, our every decision, our response to each problem was sourced from this way of being. There was a persistent pressure on us to simplify this detail to speed up the process, eliminate another detail to save costs, concede this point to pacify somebody and so on. Had we surrendered to the "reasonableness" of these demands, the building might have been completed sooner, might have cost a little less and everybody might have been happy. But the result would not be the world-class building of the original vision and the pride of all Canadians. It would not have been a symbol of the nation's quest for excellence, but a testament to the art of compromise, a testament to mediocrity. So rather than be reasonable, we were "unreasonable" and made "unreasonable" demands of everyone participating in the project.

We resisted the temptation to find solutions in logic, in expediency or in intellect. Instead, we made the most crucial decisions on the project from within this way of being. From this standpoint, we were able to see each breakdown — and there was one almost each day — as an opportunity for a breakthrough, an opportunity to enroll everyone in creating a solution.

It took an incredible team of architects, engineers, managers and technologists to achieve this, entrusted with a special responsibility. This team had to be the "source" of dedication and commitment for the project, to keep the vision alive at all times, to keep each person aligned toward the same goal. There were times when "reasonableness" and personal considerations got in the way, but in every case, we had to remind ourselves of our declared commitment to excellence, shrug off the problems — and push on. There is an awesome challenge in transforming the vision of the nation to reality, and in our service to that vision we have all been immeasurably enriched.

2. DESIGN PRINCIPLES

OBJECTIVES

The Museum will be a symbolic form. It will speak of the emergence of this continent, its forms sculptured by the winds, the rivers, the glaciers. It will speak of the emergence of man from the melting glaciers; of man and woman living in harmony with the forces of nature and evolving with them. It will show the way in which man first learned to cope with the environment, then mastered it and shaped it to the needs of his own goals and aspirations. It will depict man as a creature of the Earth who knows his tremendous power to change his environment, yet understands that he must live in harmony with it.

The building itself should truly aspire to be an artifact of our time, a celebration of man's evolution and achievement. It should point optimistically to the future, promising man's continued growth to a higher form of life, exploring not just this continent or planet but outer space as well. It should endeavour to be a spiritual act, and should demand from all those contributing to its design and construction the very best of their endeavours.

— Douglas J. Cardinal

DESIGN PHILOSOPHY

The beginning of the creative endeavour is "The Word." To bring a vision into reality, you keep your word; you keep your intention pure, which requires unwavering commitment. You operate by commitment rather than fear. Fear keeps us all powerless and small, and collapses our intentions. We have nothing to fear because we are completely connected to everyone and everything around us in the universe.

The knowledge of the universe is limitless compared to the limited knowledge of humankind. True creativity lies not in what you know, but in what you don't know.

In the vast space of the unknown, there are unlimited possibilities. One has to begin the design process without any preconceived ideas. Start from a blank sheet of paper and humbly approach the creative process from a position of not knowing. The creation of new paradigms comes from individuals who are willing to think beyond the confines of existing knowledge. Without any preconceptions I evolved a design from the inside out, open to all possibility.

Each cell or space has a particular function, like those in the human body, and my quest is to find the genetic code for each cell or space. We analyze, in depth, each space using at least 16 basic questions that must be thoroughly answered, with the responses entered into our database.

Each space is then scaled on our computers, allowing us to show samples. We also have users describe a "day in the life for each room," permitting us to understand the users' schedules, the amount of actual space they need to use and the maximum functionality they require. To conduct a detailed review for finding "the genetic code" of a space, the following steps are carried out:

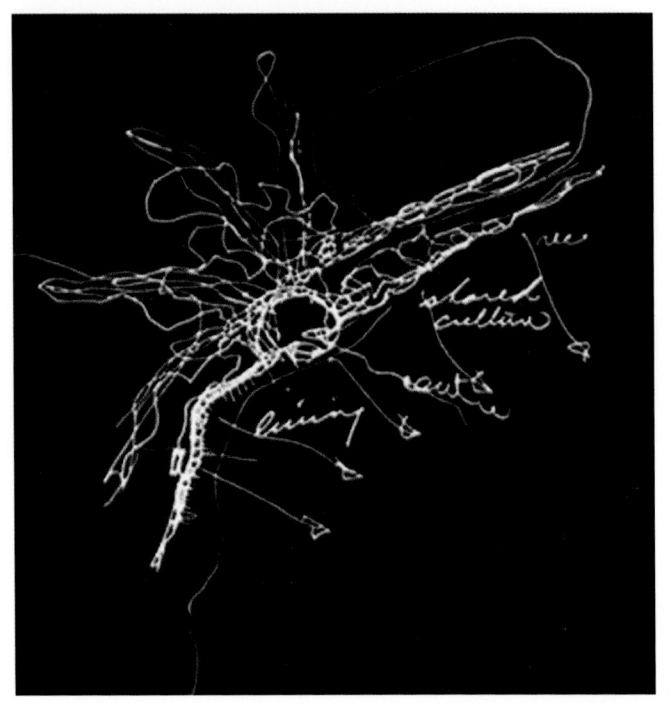

- Review the program, clarify contents of data and redevelop, as required.
- Prepare a list of all the major spaces, space sequences and interfaces.
- Analyze program requirements for all rooms in the program on a room-by-room basis.
- Establish volumetric attributes and shape options, as required for each room.
- Meet with client to establish functional criteria attributes for these rooms based on the nature of the types of exhibits to be displayed.
- Prepare a brief report about the design and layout options.
- Prepare an addendum to the functional program, including qualitative attributes for spaces determined during the vision/image sessions.
- Prepare a list of the different types of building users.
- Determine the circulation patterns and special building systems used by interviewing the user groups.
- Label the different building systems and identify the systems that relate to each room.
- Provide feedback analysis to the user groups involved to resolve building system issues.
- Incorporate feedback and insert conclusions in developing a spatial relationship matrix.

17

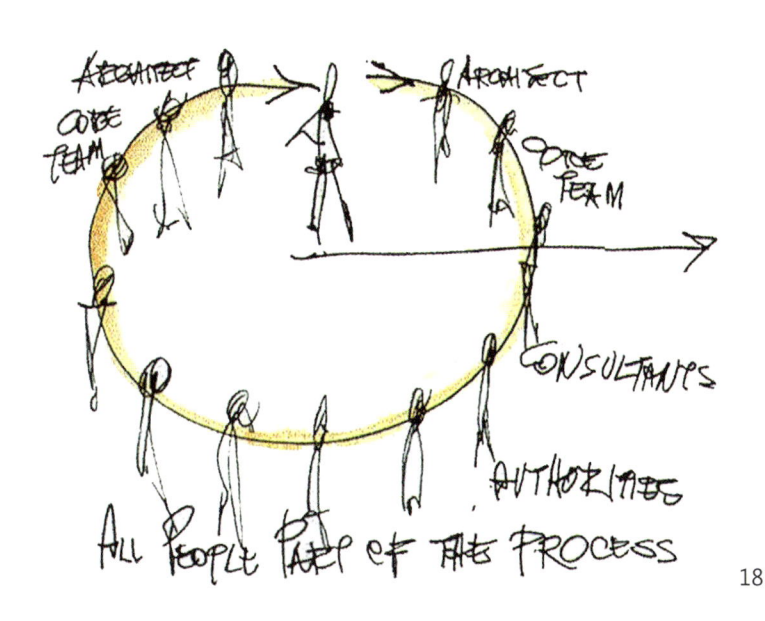

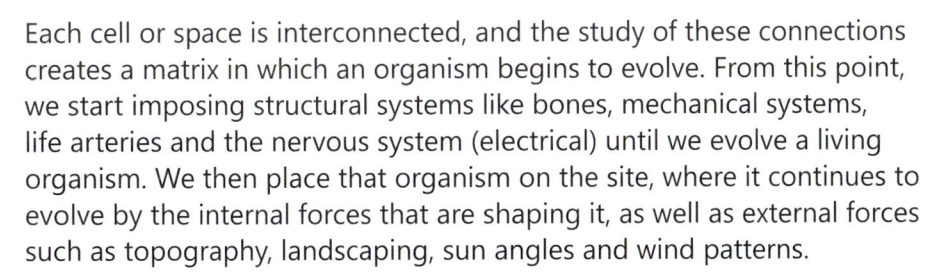

Each cell or space is interconnected, and the study of these connections creates a matrix in which an organism begins to evolve. From this point, we start imposing structural systems like bones, mechanical systems, life arteries and the nervous system (electrical) until we evolve a living organism. We then place that organism on the site, where it continues to evolve by the internal forces that are shaping it, as well as external forces such as topography, landscaping, sun angles and wind patterns.

The building evolves to satisfy all the inside and the outside forces that shape the form itself. That becomes the basis of the sculpture, which then can be pushed and shoved into a form that is a statement of the vision itself. The soft landscaping forms then flow into the hard landscaping we design.

I believe that if architecture is created with respect for the people and the environment, it can then raise the spirits of all those who are involved, as well as those who enter its spaces. Organic architecture is a natural expression of providing a beautiful environment for people in harmony with the natural environment — an expression in art of an abstraction of forms within nature, as well as our own dynamic living forms.

In architecture, I strive to elevate the human spirit and provide spaces that add drama to each function and evolve a building from the needs of the people inhabiting the spaces I create. The built environment we create should embrace and respect each individual and emphasize a respect and balance with nature.

I believe in bringing people's visions into reality.

THE DESIGN PRINCIPLES

THE BUILDING AS AN ICON

THE BUILDING AS SCULPTURAL FORM

FORM AND FUNCTION

ORIENTATION AND RELATION

PLAZAS

LANDSCAPING

ADDITIVE ARCHITECTURE

STRUCTURAL EXPRESSIONS

EXHIBITS

CROSS-REFERENCING

TECHNOLOGY

LIGHT

MATERIALS

SERVICES

THE BUILDING AS AN ICON

I would like to state my profound appreciation of the design strengths of Douglas J. Cardinal in producing the new Canadian Museum of Civilization in Hull, Quebec. The building has become a national symbol in the two years since opening. It is also achieving international acclaim as 'The Sydney Opera House of Canada' in its memorable sculptural form.

The building is also a success, in my view, in meeting the very high performance requirements of a museum with priceless and very fragile collections of literally millions of objects. The architect was most responsive to the requirements expressed in our architectural programme and has produced a facility that has set a new standard in the museological world.

I personally feel the value for dollar of our investment in the building is an excellent one in comparison with like structures here and abroad that I have examined, and one that will continue to serve the needs of Canada as a treasure house for its historical collection for centuries to come.

I found Douglas Cardinal to be a most creative individual to work with throughout the seven years he devoted to the project and recommend his abilities to deliver a major project at reasonable cost and lasting value without qualifications.

— Dr. George F. MacDonald
Director, Canadian Museum of Civilization
1991

THE BUILDING AS SCULPTURAL FORM

The building has a very strong horizontal motif with sinuous curves that represent the natural landscaping found along the Ottawa River. The impression I wanted to create was one of stratified layers of the Earth's crust carved by water and wind. The building's forms step back so they do not oppose the landscaping but flow into it.

On the plaza side, I designed the forms to overhang and cantilever over the plaza area like a natural cliff that has been slowly carved by water over time. I wanted to give the visitors a feeling of protection and shelter while in the plaza. If it started to rain, people could walk close to the building to protect themselves. Overall, I wanted the building to be more Ionic, more feminine, as a protective nurturing space that envelops the public. This way the public would have more empathy towards the building's forms, and the building's forms would show more empathy toward the public. I designed this structure so that the roofs could be converted into green roofs in the future, then the roofs themselves could be landscaped. All of the mechanical equipment and roof accesses are designed as stone sculptural forms, which tie into the sculptural, sinuous shapes of both the upper and lower plazas that flow down into the riverbanks. Future buildings on Laurier Street will be able to see across the Museum to Parliament Hill, while having full view of these sculptural roof forms instead of mechanical boxes.

21

22

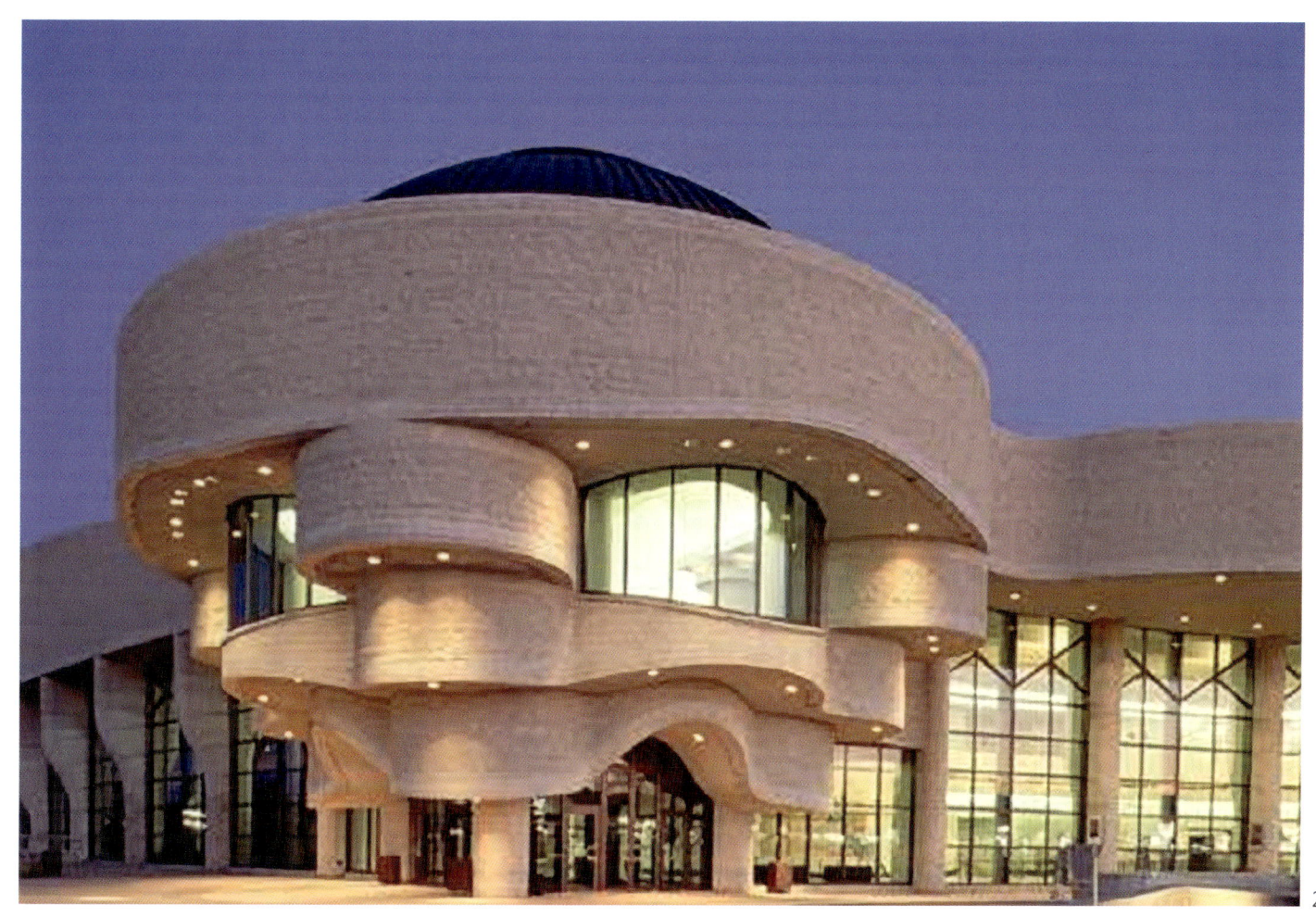

FORM AND FUNCTION

I am pleased that the architecture of the buildings will take advantage of the surrounding landscape. Their esthetics will certainly help to emphasize their key role in the cultural life of Canadians.

— Francis Fox
Minister, Department of Communications
(During the unveiling of architectural models of the new Museum)
November 28, 1983

After being selected as principal architect for the project, I was presented with a program that defined all the spaces and functions, including interior layouts and some volume estimates. With my team's careful analysis of the required spaces, combined with thorough discussions with the staff members of the Museum, we were able to clarify in detail the necessary points for the design. These program clarifications added up to two additional volumes of detailed information that supplemented the existing four volumes of the program. On that basis, we started to develop the rooms, or cells, of this organic structure, following the very clear description of how each space related to one another to develop a matrix of relationships that functioned according to George MacDonald and his staff.

All of the spaces are designed to flow into one another, and the sculptural forms are curvilinear, so visitors cannot deliberately define the space as they move from one area to another. The building keeps unfolding and, by changing the cross-referencing of the halls, it adds to the desire for one space to flow into another. Using a series of sinuous S-shaped curves creates a more dynamic form. The entrance is designed to be a pavilion-head open in all directions, making the entrance a strong sculptural form and the main feature of the plaza.

Within the plaza, the Grand Hall stretches along the main axis of the building in a series of ramps and cascading waterfalls that beckon visitors to the water's edge at the other end. Here visitors experience the rebirth of life on this planet from the melting waters of the receding glaciers. The convoluted swirls shaped by glacial action are reflected in the rounded, sinuous forms. The melting waters are seen in the sparkling water that starts as a small stream at the top of the plaza, criss-crosses its way between the ramps and grows to a cascade as it reaches the pools at the lower end.

This is an internal urban park on a human scale, to be enjoyed year-round. The ramps and levels of the building resemble a carving that shows the influence of the elements and the water in their shapes and forms. The building's roof captures the sun's rays from dawn to dusk, bending shafts of sunlight downward. The water of the West Coast is represented by the polished granite set in elongated curves along the whole expression of the Grand Hall. The different grading of the granite symbolizes the crests of rippling waves as they would crash into the shore. The artificial rock-like formations at the edge of the wooden boardwalk transition to the stylized edge of the coastal line, another example of the integration of exhibit and architecture.

23

ORIENTATION AND RELATION

After crossing the Alexandra Bridge, the major street is Boulevard des Allumettières, which intersects with Laurier Street. At such a prominent location, I established a vision cone that would respect and capture views of the Parliament Buildings. A second vision cone was created to respect the view from the City Hall of Hull to Parliament Hill. The vision cone from the plaza required the Grand Hall to be at the appropriate angle, more northeast because the Grand Hall needed to address the river and Parliament Hill. In this location, I had more control over the natural lighting than if the Grand Hall was facing south.

Influenced by the Spanish Steps in Rome as a centre for activities on different levels, I designed the plaza to function similarly. People could use the steps like an amphitheatre to view functions and events on the lower plaza levels, as well as the fireworks from across the river at Parliament Hill. I also felt it was important to create a balcony around the space at the Laurier Street level and at the roof of the restaurant, which would not only present views of the lower plaza, but also the Ottawa River and Parliament Hill.

From the Laurier Street level the building had two prominent masses and, since the site sloped to the river, there was an opportunity to have a whole level below Laurier Street facing the Ottawa River. This creates a lower plaza, which surrounds the building on three sides, with one side opening to the park along the river. The Laurier Street level and the river level are situated next to a grand stair and waterfalls to create a gathering space for functions and celebrations.

27

28

None of the nearby public buildings truly addressed the river, which is one of the most beautiful and natural resources in the Ottawa Valley. I wanted the design to address the river and Parliament Hill at every opportunity.

29

For example, in joining the Grand Hall with other public spaces (including meeting rooms, library and cafeteria), I felt it was fundamental to take full advantage of the dramatic view of the river and the Parliament Buildings. Consequently, as visitors pass from the Grand Hall under the waterfall, they have a special view of Parliament Hill. As they walk under the stairs again, the walkway to the cafeteria opens to the lower plaza and the river. The cafeteria and outside eating area take full advantage of the magnificent view, displaying the National Gallery, Parliament Hill, the Supreme Court of Canada and all the great historical monuments, including the Rideau Canal locks, the Château Laurier hotel, the Confederation Buildings and the sacred Anishinabe Island (Victoria Island). It is a beautiful, dramatic view representing the history of Canada. Such a wondrous vista should also be seen from the roof of the restaurant, which initially I designed as a pavilion. In fact, I initially designed all the roofs, including the roof over the Grand Hall and other exhibit areas, to be green, along with some of the roofs over the administration area, which are now landscaped.

PLAZAS

Placing all these programmatic functions onsite created major changes to the initial forms. In addition, the site also had to address the francophone community of Hull, the anglophone community of Ottawa and the Ottawa River. Fundamental to my concept was that this public building should not become a wall between these two communities. It is also important to note that the site was previously a park where the francophone community used to access to the river. I believed it was imperative to keep that relationship intact.

30

I therefore designed the plaza facing Laurier Street for the francophone community and separated the building masses, which are joined together at a lower level so the francophone community would still have total access to the river at all times. Conversely, the plaza, in concept, would flow all the way to the river shore with cascading stairs and water, so from the plaza a visitor would have a dramatic view of Parliament Hill.

LANDSCAPING

I regard the whole site as landscaping: hard landscaping in the building, sidewalks, plazas and bicycle trails; and soft landscaping in the grass, trees and foliage. When I design, I have the building design flow into the landscaping design and vice versa so there is not an exact line between the building and landscaping — they are completely integrated.

I initially planned the roofs to be landscaped and accessible to the public, where there could be sculptural gardens or artifacts that could withstand our climate. The landscape architect worked with me in Alberta and he understood that it was very important for the design of the landscaping (particularly the geometry of the layout) to coincide with the design of my building. We collaborated very closely regarding the forms, textures and types of plants and layout that would be suitable for the site and follow my design themes.

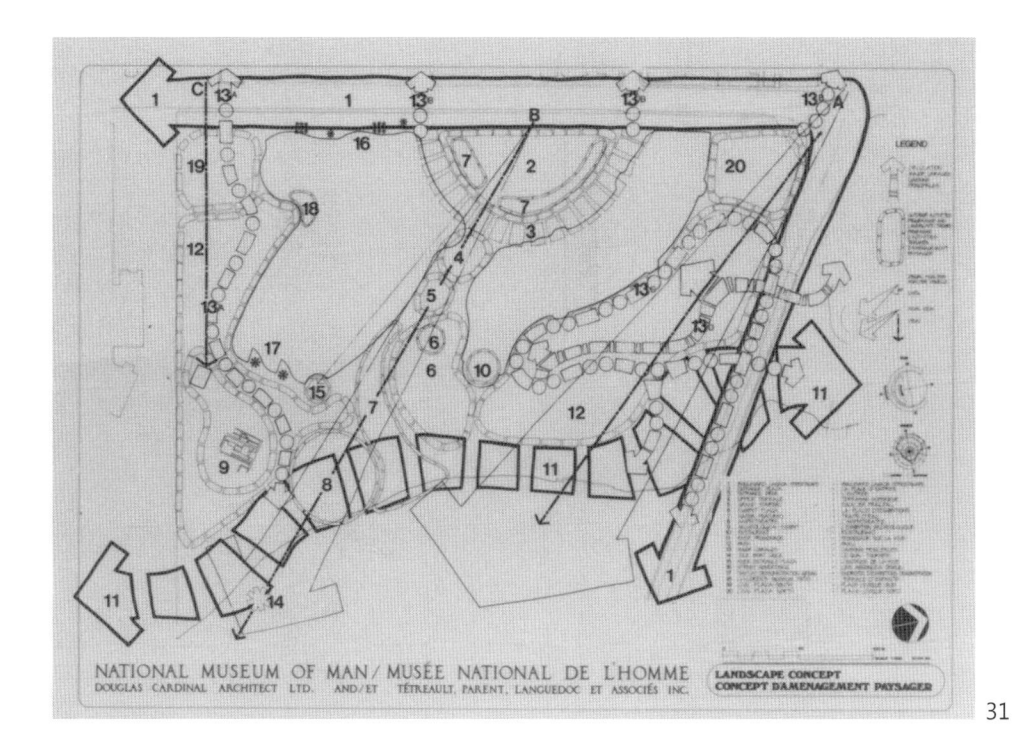

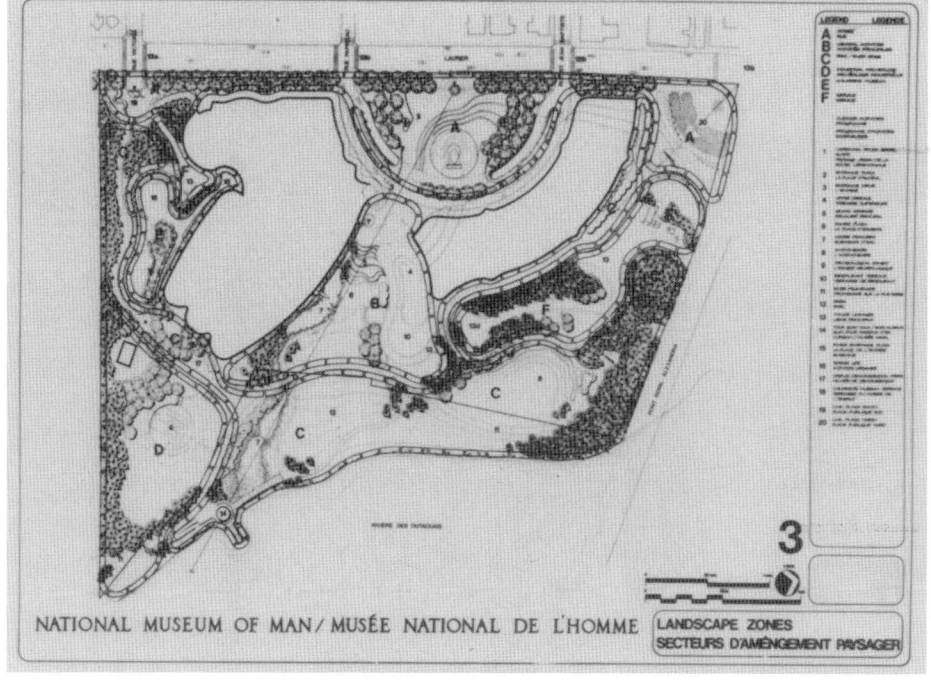

33

34

35

ADDITIVE ARCHITECTURE

Railings, Stairs and Sculptures
The handrails and exterior balustrades had to follow the sensuous curves of the building and flow into each other in a seamless, organic composition. I emphasized these forms with contrasting cut stone and rough cut stone, laid in a variety of setting beds to emulate the natural strata of the earth.

The Grand Hall is three levels tall in order to incorporate the beautiful totem poles — one of the finest collections in the world. The Grand Hall allows the opportunity of creating a West Coast village with different house fronts from various West Coast First Nations. These monumental forms of the West Coast, as well as the sculptures by Bill Reid, complement the monumental architecture, which was also inspired by nature.

STRUCTURAL EXPRESSIONS

General

The highly curvilinear forms of the building, such as the main entrance element, demanded an imaginative use of concrete formwork. Although the concrete is covered with stone, a low degree of tolerance was permitted by the intricate geometry. The sophisticated CAD systems that my team used allowed us to generate geometrical data to the necessary level of detail.

Concrete Skeleton

The use of concrete enabled the design of the striking cantilevers for Block B, the curatorial wing, where a flat-slab system was adopted to provide the maximum possible headroom for artifact storage and handling. By adapting the building to accommodate the later design of fit-up exhibits, my team took advantage of the extra strength in concrete for retrofit work, such as adding extra floors, increasing design loads, modifying the skeleton shape, etc. The versatility and adaptability of concrete played a crucial role in facilitating several other last-minute changes necessitated by the fast-track method.

Precast concrete was used to provide the structural support for stone in the "humps" of the Grand Hall columns. While the straight (lower) portions of the columns consist of stone cladding supported directly off the steel structure, the "humps" (upper) consist of stone cladding that was cast integrally with a specially shaped concrete backing in a precast concrete plant in Winnipeg. Detail drawings at a ratio of 1:1 were used to accurately build each column. Afterward, these stone-clad curved segments were transported whole to the job site and then hoisted into place.

EXHIBITS

The cataloguing, conservation and workshop area for creating exhibits is adjacent to the collections holding area. Between collections and exhibit construction, there is a corridor under the Laurier Street level that connects the Curatorial and Museum buildings. Large elevators are able to distribute the collections to the various levels and provide access along the main artifact route to the exhibit areas. The large elevators from the exhibit areas also carry the exhibits to three levels of the exhibition halls.

To assist with controlling the environment of the collection's holding levels, it was imperative to protect the interior walls from the changing outside climate. Artifacts need a constant temperature and humidity or they will deteriorate, and these sensitive objects cannot tolerate temperature variations of more than 2° Celsius or humidity fluctuations over 5 percent. To protect the collections, we wrapped the corridors and staff offices around the perimeter of the collections as a buffer. The purpose was two-fold. First, the buffer gave staff members an exterior view because a variety of light and views of the changing environment outside help people function better. Second, the buffer between the outside walls and the walls around the collections makes it easier for the artifacts to be housed at a constant temperature.

Every space that has artifacts is designed with very rigid environmental conditions, such as 50 percent relative humidity and a temperature of 22° Celsius with very little variation, in accordance with the Canadian Conservation Institute. Primarily these spaces were designed similarly to an operating room, and special care was taken to have the same temperature and humidity throughout the space, including the floor-to-ceiling space of the Grand Hall. I worked out the engineering concepts with Cosentini Associates of New York, who have experience designing museums around the world, including The Field Museum in Chicago, the Metropolitan Museum in New York and the Smithsonian in Washington, D.C.

In the changing exhibit halls, we developed a coffered ceiling that was approximately 2 metres by 2 metres, and each coffer had controlled environmental conditions (sensors) so we could create changing exhibits with more flexibility in the layout and the protection of the artifacts. Initially, we had a First Nations gallery, because the National Gallery of Canada did not accept Aboriginal artists in the 1980s (not accepting it as fine art). The National Gallery of Canada now proudly exhibits Aboriginal work.

The archaeology collections require less environmental control because they are mostly rocks and fossils. Consequently, they are able to be placed in the upper level where temperatures might fluctuate due to the roof above. The space of the collection holding areas is two stories high, allowing mezzanines to be built to efficiently store all the artifacts. The building is designed so constant airflow, temperature and humidity can be introduced at each level, including the mezzanine levels.

The administration area primarily faces Parliament Hill and the Grand Hall. The administrative office of the President and CEO, along with the boardroom, have a full view of the Parliament Buildings, the Ottawa River, Victoria Island and the upper and lower plazas of the Museum.

The vaulted ceilings in the Canada Hall and the First Peoples Hall can be used as projection surfaces to further enhance the exhibits, particularly the Grand Hall, which has been the location of many official dinners with heads of state, including Her Majesty Queen Elizabeth II. The Grand Hall transforms into a projection surface to imitate water, fire or any other desired symbols to highlight an event; for example, stars and stripes to honour a visit by the President of the United States.

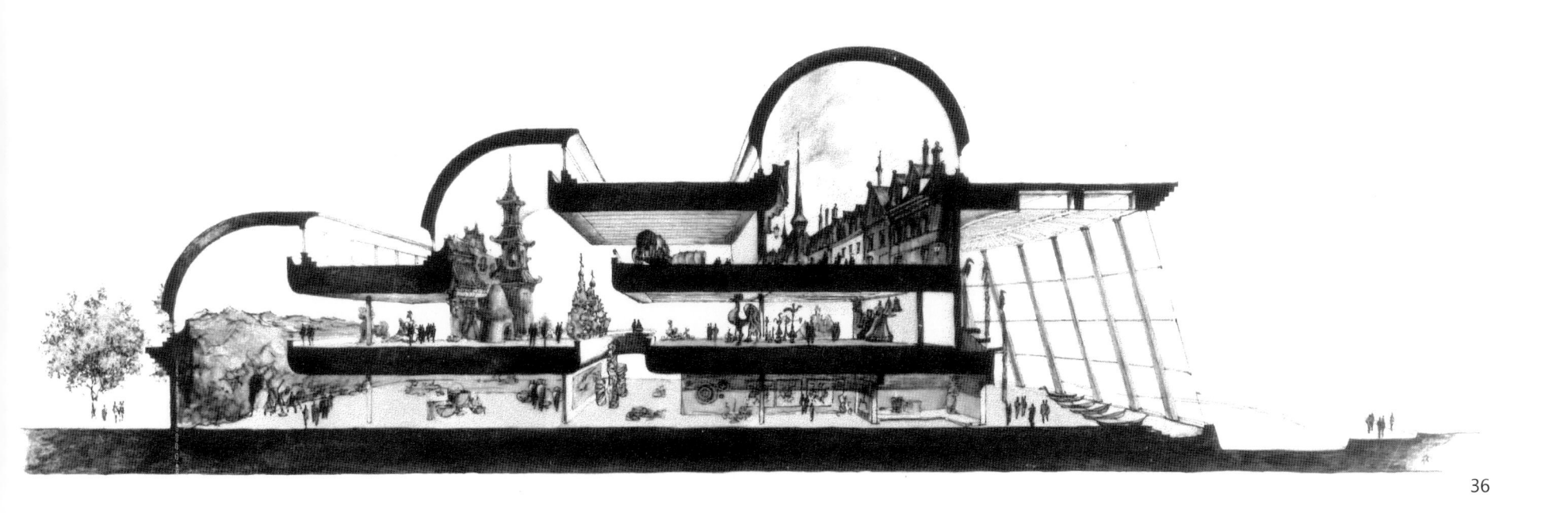

CROSS-REFERENCING

Entry and exit from the exhibit halls are from the Grand Hall and, whether entering or leaving a hall, visitors can always orient themselves to the building. All the halls were designed for cross-referencing, so a visitor could look into the halls at various levels. This allows the visitor to not only see the exhibits in that particular space, but also look into other spaces at different levels, which entices and raises curiosity to see other exhibits. It was very important for the exhibit designer to have these specially designed exhibits that would encourage visitors to continue their journey by drawing them into the different spaces.

TECHNOLOGY

The Museum is one of the world's most advanced buildings in its use of high technology and, when it was completed in 1989, set new standards for museum design.

The building, covering an area of some 1 million square feet, or 15 million cubic feet, houses a wide variety of uses, each with its own unique requirements: exhibit areas, collections holding rooms with high-security vaults, an auditorium, a movie theatre, curatorial laboratories, workshops, administrative offices, lounges, restaurants and cafeterias.

The building stores Canada's most precious articles under highly controlled environmental conditions and, at the same time, exhibits them to the public under unprecedented conditions of openness and celebration. Unique solutions were created for air-handling systems to provide a uniform "laminar" air flow in artifact areas and maintain environmental conditions, even with frequent changes in occupancy conditions.

An integrated data and communications network was provided using state-of-the-art fibre optics technology. This network includes more than 30 separate systems for voice and data communications, interlinking not only all of the building's internal systems, but also interlinking the Museum with the systems of other museums across Canada. There is enough communications cabling in the building to wrap around the world 22 times!

For the public's entertainment, the building has a CINÉ+ movie theatre, which contains two major systems within one space: the flat screen (measuring some 25 metres across and 20 metres high), as well as the domed screen (measuring 23 metres in diameter). Each screen is capable of being moved to make room for the other. The flat screen folds into a trench in the floor, while the dome can lift and slide out of sight above and behind the audience. The high optical precision and total vibration control needed in this theatre are achieved in its structural and acoustical design.

The design uses elevator technology with cables and appropriate braking systems for the large dome screen. Volumes of chilled air, which is cooled because it is designed for an interior space seating some 300 people, are directed downward and the return air is taken from behind the seats, so the air system is an air sweep designed to filter fine particles of dust out of the air and not interfere with the projection of the images on the dome, which has 15 percent perforations for sound and sprinkler systems.

The Museum's theatre is 8:16:32 projection with translating booths, as well as a system of variable acoustics, allowing the flexibility for film, theatre and music in the space. The theatre can also be used as a television studio to broadcast events and has access to a loading dock for special stage requirements.

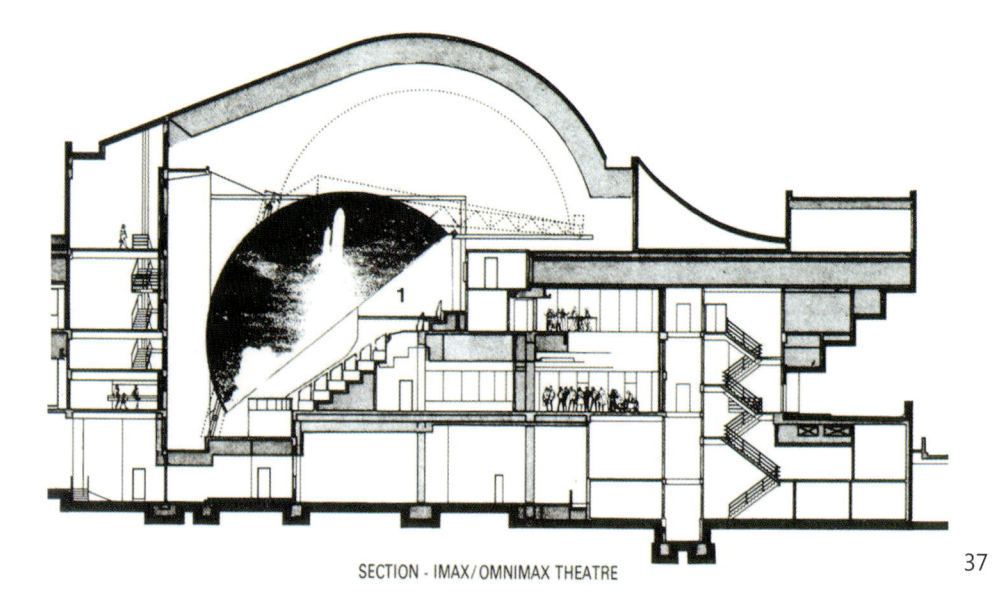

SECTION - IMAX/OMNIMAX THEATRE

LIGHT

The galleries are designed for natural light (through those clerestory spaces), although all the natural light is designed to reflect off the ceilings and become indirect lighting in the galleries. The indirect light is augmented by artificial light. The galleries were not intended to be black boxes, which is definitely a mistake in many museums because there is no shape or ambience to black box halls. Natural daylight has been admitted to many areas that house the artifacts, and the ultraviolet rays of the light have been filtered to almost zero-level through the use of special glazing in the skylights and clerestories, and specially constituted paints on interior surfaces.

The ceilings were an opportunity to create dramatic designs because the floors and walls are primarily planned for exhibits. There are just a few opportunities to create artistic and sculptural exhibits on the ceiling, which provide great opportunities for the architect to create sculptural forms. Working with Lamb and Associates from New York, we developed lighting systems that worked with the ceilings and curvilinear slots, which allowed us to have more dramatic ceilings and add colour, as well.

We visited selected major museums around the world, including the British Museum in London, the Louvre in Paris, the Metropolitan Museum in New York, Topkapi Palace in Istanbul, St. Peter's in Rome and many others. In our detailed conversations and research with the museum's directors, exhibit personnel and programmers, we were advised that the public did not like exhibit displays in black boxes. Indeed, the public on many occasions would not even enter a museum space where the concept of the exhibit hall was a black box. They mentioned that exhibition designers like the flexibility of black boxes because they could put the lights, projectors, speakers, security systems, etc. in any location in the black ceiling, which visually obscures any systems that are disorderly or inconsistent.

During my research, the special lighting consultants said that the public prefers a higher level of light in a space. It is important, however, to protect the artifacts with very low lighting. But low lighting in a black box makes the space too dark and uninviting. A space is more welcoming and inviting, and can still have low lighting for the artifacts, if the walls and the ceilings are lit. To achieve this, the lighting consultants, who were internationally known to have the best expertise, recommended that we put the lighting in slots in the ceiling to hide all the pipes, sprinklers, mechanical systems, etc., which are usually painted black in a black box gallery. These slots in the ceiling, which are about 2 metres apart, create the flexibility for exhibit design.

Using slots also allows the ceiling to be finished and painted in any colour. The ceilings become a very important element in the design because the floor and walls are filled with exhibits and the ceilings themselves then become very strong architectural statements.

From my research, people related far more to spaces where they could feel the overall form of the hall as an architectural background rather than a black box, which did not define the feeling of the space at all. The lighting consultant wanted the slots in the ceiling to be as narrow as possible and designed lights that could swing from the front of the light fixture rather than from the back of the fixture, allowing us to have a narrower slot for the lights. This is why all the ceilings in the First Peoples Hall have curvilinear slots to create a more dramatic ceiling, allowing the ceiling to have different colours to enhance the space. The lighting consultant recommended a narrow slot with panels that could be opened on either side to adjust the lights, speakers and any other systems that need to be directed to the artifacts in the exhibits. The 2 meter by 2 meter pipe grid above the ceiling could have exhibits attached through these slots as well. This was an improvement in the overall design.

MATERIALS

Rather than using a variety of materials and textures to create interest and vitality, I concentrated on using form and sculpture in the floors, walls and ceilings of each space. Colours and materials are easily dated, but monumental forms and sculpture can be timeless. I looked at every opportunity on surfaces to magnify the sculptural form.

The roofs are sculptural forms composed of copper, since copper and stone are the main materials in the historical buildings on the other side of the river, such as Victoria Island (the sacred Anishinabe Island), the Parliament Buildings, the Confederation Buildings and the Supreme Court building.

The design of the building is conceived as a sculptural statement representing the natural forms of the Canadian landscape, symbolizing the backbone of our continent. To depict this, I selected stone as the primary material. Tyndall stone is a natural-quarried, light coloured, mottled, dolomitic limestone. It is a subdivision of the Western Canadian Sedimentary Basin quarried near Tyndall, Manitoba by Gillis Quarries Ltd. The mottled colour is caused by the burrowing of marine creatures when the limestone was deposited. It also contains numerous gastropod, brachiopod, cephalopod, trilobite, coral and stromatoporoid fossils.

41

SERVICES

Initially, food and garbage were to be totally separated from any area with artifacts, although there was a provision to have banquets in the Grand Hall. I therefore designed the restaurant and cafeteria to address the river and Parliament Hill, as well as the upper and lower plazas. The cafeteria was designed so people could flow outside and enjoy the river and the views when the weather permitted, and trees were chosen that were more like shading umbrellas. The south orientation extends the time frame that visitors can enjoy the outside. Walking from the Grand Hall to the cafeteria, underneath the stairs and waterfalls, I wanted the meeting rooms and library to be very exciting spaces that encouraged people to participate in these major functions. All the ceilings, floors and walls of the interior were designed in sensuous curves to accent the architecture. The lighting was indirect and in coves to accent the architecture. The mechanical systems, as well, were hidden, and the grills were inconspicuous in coves.

The mechanics and lighting were minor elements hidden in the architectural forms (e.g., speakers, electronics, sprinkler heads, and any other paraphernalia), and were designed not to detract from architectural lines of the building.

The administration and collection holding building faces the Alexandra Bridge, and the challenge was to hide from the bridge and Parliament Hill any sight of the trucks, service vehicles and the large loading docks for shipping and receiving and garbage areas. The large overhang over the service area makes the entire service area fairly invisible, which is then even more disguised by evergreen landscaping.

All the service traffic is under the bridge and is shielded from Parliament Hill by a large earth ramp that joins the bicycle route along the river to the Laurier Street level above the river level. This bicycle route connects to Laurier Street, as well as the restaurant level. Laurier Street was widened to create Confederation Boulevard, which would be a major circle joining the francophone, anglophone and Aboriginal communities in a dramatic circle where the future public buildings would be showcased, symbolically joining Canada itself with the river.

Underneath the plaza is the bus drop-off and public parking. The plaza, including the landscaping, was designed with sinuous curves, echoing the sinuous curves of the building. These lines flow into the building forms themselves and abstractly run into the landscaping. Care must be taken so the landscape forms do not block the dramatic view of Parliament Hill between the two building masses. The building masses are separated into two: curatorial collections holding and administration areas next to the bridge and exhibit galleries in the west block. As stated earlier, the service areas are accessed under the bridge. The shipping and receiving areas are adjacent to the conservation areas.

The concept for the mechanical system was to primarily use the river water to heat and cool the building; only for a few months in the winter are fossil fuels needed to supplement the heating source. The water comes from the Ottawa River where, with large heat pumps or chillers, calories are taken out of the water to heat and cool the building. Heating and cooling water is transferred to some 150 units distributed throughout the Museum complex. The units are placed in humidity zones, and humidity migrates through these zones. The units also have fresh air distributed to each of them; the necessary humidity and fresh air is taken from the outside air, then filtered and enhanced or reduced in temperature and humidity as necessary by coils. The coils receive their cooling source from chillers and their heat source from the heat rejected by the same chillers located in the central heating and cooling plant of the Museum.

The exhaust system vents the air from restaurants, washrooms and other spaces, as required. Computers monitor the fresh air, the humidity and the heating and cooling water to each unit. The units supply hot air, cold air, fresh air and humidity to a series of mixing boxes throughout the zone. The mixing boxes combine the air and humidity to exact requirements and distribute the air throughout that zone. The mixing box is digitally controlled by the computer so even if a crowd of people enter and let off higher temperatures and humidity, sensors throughout the zone will adjust the mixing box accordingly. As a result, no matter how many people are in the spaces, the temperature will adjust to the changing environment. There is a separate system that heats the exterior building shell. It also blows air across every panel of glass so no humidity will build up on the exterior, triple-glazed glass, particularly in areas such as the Grand Hall, or disrupt the clerestory natural light in the galleries.

There is electrical power in the lower floor ducts every 2 metres, and there are accessible plugs in the floor slabs of the second and third levels every 2 metres both ways. At a thousand points in the Museum, there is a universal communication outlet of fibre optics and copper that connects to a main panel in the library area, where all of the fibre optic cables are all home runs, so appliances could be attached at both ends of the cables for the life of the building.

3. THE FUTURE

When the building (is) carried above the footprints to the walls and roofs, as you see them in the model, it will also be discovered how thoughtful the architect (has) been of its neighbours. They have kept their building low, out of respect for those... who will build in the future, for example, across Laurier Street....

— Jean Sutherland Boggs
Chair, Canada Museums Construction Corporation
November 28, 1983

DOUGLAS CARDINAL'S GENERAL DESIGN PRINCIPLES

INSPIRATION
Nature — Trust in the Forms
Human

PURPOSE
Connect with All
Harmonize and Flow

TECHNIQUE
In Problem-Solving

A BUILDING AS A SYMBOL
Land
Water
Cultural — Canadian
Multicultural Celebration
Canoes and Boats
Materials
Vision

THE MUSEUM AS HISTORICAL ART

FORM AND FUNCTION
Everything Should Flow
The Techniques of the Curves
Materials
Additional Architectural Elements

ORIENTATION AND FLOW
The Ottawa River
Flow
No Black Boxes
Visitor Experience

SETTING AND MEANING

CONCLUSION

DOUGLAS CARDINAL'S GENERAL DESIGN PRINCIPLES

INSPIRATION

Nature — Trust in the Forms
I always believed if you do timeless organic forms, they can never be dated. I derive the forms from nature, which are eternal and develop the forms that relate to the human body.

Forms based on nature are timeless.

We have been developing these organic forms since the beginning of time.

Douglas Cardinal's inspiration in nature relies on the geographical and environmental formations of the Earth itself. Yet, the power of Cardinal's lines is that the forms are not copies of nature; he never tries to emulate nature or recreate nature in his buildings.

All forms I design are abstractions of nature.

The abstract forms that I derive from nature are from water and earth, carved by the forces of nature herself.

The abstraction of nature is the most sophisticated manner society has devised to balance the human built environments into organic, proportionate human scale. Unlike the Babylonians and Egyptians, the Greeks created architecture on a human scale based on the harmony and proportions of nature.

Hills and valleys intertwined with the forms of our male and female bodies. Like the Greeks of the past, I relate my forms to nature.

For Cardinal, the originality of abstracting natural forms comes from the unique Canadian landscape. It is this inspiration that has created a magnificent and modern aesthetic based on strong emotional connection with the Canadian landscape.

I am inspired by the strong, organic, natural and curvilinear spaces that grow out of the landscape. Like Lawren Harris of the Group of Seven, I see that the powerful forms of nature are truly the inspiration of my architectural expression.

Human
But the inspiration of nature is not limited to the natural environment and physical forms of the planet. Particularly important for harmony is our interaction with nature, as our own bodies, as natural organisms, are an intrinsic part of nature itself.

I intertwined the male and female forms with nature because my expression as an artist is to illustrate that we are all connected to each other and connected to all nature around us.

PURPOSE

Connect With All

The inspiration of nature in Cardinal's architecture is not merely aesthetic. There is a deeper reason. The purpose is to help the human psyche harmonize with nature itself. Instead of fighting it and trying to control it, Cardinal strives to honour and thrive in expressing that we humans are an intrinsic part of nature.

It is not simply the form, but the principle, the intention of nature. In nature all is connected.

Rather than seeing nature as a series of contrasting forms and shapes, I abstract these forms to flow together. I regard nature in the spiritual way, where everything is connected; everything is in balance and harmony, and we human beings are an intrinsic part of nature. We are connected to nature and are part of nature's balance and harmony, which flow through our own bodies.

Harmonize and Flow

The architecture materializes as an organic expression of nature's values of connectedness. Cardinal's buildings therefore not only sit harmoniously in a landscape, but also create a sense of well-being when one is inside the building.

My forms flow into each other. The curves of my buildings are sinuous curves that are all connected to each other. These curves flow inside the building to the exterior of the building and into the landscape.

TECHNIQUE

Nature is never capricious; there is logic, reason and, ultimately, a purpose with every element and organism on the planet. When abstracting nature, the same kind of rigorous discipline needs to be applied; otherwise we just mimic nature instead of bringing the essence of its principles.

These curves are not broken or separate from each other. The lines are flowing and interconnected based on strict geometry.

In Problem-Solving

All solutions are in nature. The most advanced organic solutions are working in nature. For Cardinal, the solution is simple: all one needs is the technology of computers and creativity to abstract that knowledge.

I think that where there are complications, there is an opportunity to create complex design solutions that seem to grow out of these problems — an organic solution.

A BUILDING AS A SYMBOL

Land

The Museum is a monument to reflect the singular variety of the Canadian landscape.

The building is a reflection of the rocks that form this continent, which are carved over time by the water and the wind.

The main plaza welcomes the visitor where the building cantilevers itself to the plaza as cliffs.

Water

Water is the foundation of life on the planet. Thus a building that reflects and is inspired by water and its forms reflects the absolute connectedness of all creatures on the planet.

The water symbol is an expression of life emerging from the female form of the curatorial wing and the male form of the exhibit wing.

All lines should follow the patterns and inspiration of flowing water. That is the main theme of the building's harmonics.

Particularly because of its setting close to the river, the water and the rich waterways of Canada are an inspiration for the building and its landscaped forms.

The lines of the building are continuous across the whole site in a sinuous pattern that abstractly represents the Ottawa River that flows through this whole region of Canada.

Sinuously flow toward the Ottawa River.

The symbols of form sculpted by water are a theme through the design.

Cultural — Canadian
The Museum is designed to become a cultural symbol in itself based on Canadian values; a symbol of expanding harmonious relationships in our unique human landscape.

We are all connected with each other and our beautiful Canadian dramatic landscape.

The building is majestically set to relate to both physical and sociocultural achievements of the land that is Canada, savouring and expressing the physical beauty of the river bank and culture by allowing a view of the spectacular buildings showcasing Canada's accomplishments as a nation.

The lines of the plaza lead you to the main entrance, to the portico between the buildings and to the lower plaza with cascading fountains and steps to the landscape to view the Ottawa River, the Rideau Canal, Parliament and other great buildings of Canada.

Multicultural Celebration
The landscaping and architectural elements that lead the visitor to the Ottawa River are designed for celebration.

From these steps, inspired by the Spanish Staircase in Rome, the lower plaza could be surrounded by people and performers. That space between the two buildings would be the gathering space for many people to celebrate their cultures outside.

This spirit of celebration is also represented in the interior, particularly the Grand Hall.

The Grand Hall is a gathering and celebration space bringing people together; connecting them to the Parliament Buildings and the other historical buildings across the river, and to the beautiful natural assets of the Ottawa River itself.

Canoes and Boats
But the building goes further in abstracting the essence of the cultures that gather to celebrate the riches of Canada. Again water, the waterways and the way humans have navigated became a symbol and tribute to the unique cultural development in Canada.

The Grand Hall is the symbol of the canoes, boats and ships that have brought peoples to all parts of Canada through the waterways.

Materials
The material of the building itself symbolizes the connection with nature.

The curving exterior walls are made from Tyndall stone, which is composed of the first life of the planet from a quarry in central Canada.

Furthermore, culturally the stone connects with the most important symbol of Canadian identity: the Parliament Buildings.

Using this material connects the building to Parliament, which uses the same stone throughout its interiors. The copper domes and vaults also relate to the copper roofs of the Parliament Buildings.

Vision
Ultimately the Museum represents a vision of Canadian unity. It was a national symbol envisioned by one prime minister that was built through the fiscal efforts of another. The Museum thus represents the best of what happens when the nation works beyond politics toward the goal of serving the Canadian culture and landscape at large.

For the National Museum, Prime Minister Pierre Trudeau saw this artistic expression as a way to speak to every person of this country because we all have come here to share the land and its resources.

THE MUSEUM AS HISTORICAL ART

The Museum is a work of art, a sculpture of wondrous forms and rich statements. The architecture needed to express the complex mission of representing a vision that transcended cultures, time and space.

It was imperative to me to rely on the sculptural forms and the architectural statement of the vision.

The building is so singular and meaningful that it has received many civic and architectural awards, including the Order of Canada for Douglas Cardinal and gold medals for architecture in Canada and Russia. Such recognition should be respected in perpetuity.

There should be provisions for the acknowledgment and continuity of Cardinal's vision and intention in evaluating future work on the Canadian Museum of History.

I frankly feel that someone who truly understands the language of my architecture and expression should be involved in any future works on the Museum. The person who I entrust with this task is my wife and partner, Idoia Arana-Beobide de Cardinal.

To value and acknowledge the art, the forms should be respected and honoured.

The building forms should be devoid of distracting elements such as hanging signs, lights or any other paraphernalia that is usually attached to buildings. I wanted nothing to distract from the strong sculptural shapes and form of the Museum.

FORM AND FUNCTION

The curves and sinuous forms of the Museum are symbolic and, as such, deemed capricious. Quite the contrary, the curves are deeply imbedded in careful mathematical execution because abstracting natural forms requires rigorous geometry, composition and calculation. As in a ballet, the result becomes sinuous, flowing lines that continuously unwind as the visitor moves through the building. The lines are carefully projected in a continuous pull by the sighting, feeling and movement.

Everything Should Flow

The lines should flow. The spaces should flow into one another; one space should pull you into another space.

Every curve relates to another curve in a continuous, sinuous manner.

The Technique of the Curves

All the curves of the Museum, although continuous, are geometric arches of circles, and all these circles have a geometric pattern that can only be truly understood by someone trained in music counterpoint and harmony, and designs in organic principles of architecture incorporated by the Friends of Kebyar.

Any protruding forms or any additions, or any modification to take away parts of the Museum, should be done in a way that synchronizes with sculptural, sinuous curves as they would blend harmoniously with the composition.

In the future, great care should be taken when adding or changing the design concepts of the Museum so the objective and flow of the building and the visitors' experience remains as powerful as originally intended.

If and when needed, adding or modifying any interior forms should follow the sensuous forms of the building and not stand out as separate elements, but feel very much a part of the architecture so the spaces retain their flow.

Materials
The materials of the architecture are simplified on purpose to create cohesiveness. This way, the architecture is a free-standing sculpture remaining as neutral as possible in the display of the many colourful artifacts. This also prevents the visitor from becoming overwhelmed by abundant contradicting forms, shapes and colours.

I simplified all the exterior finishes to stone, glass and copper rather than a variety of other building materials, which would distract from the sculptural statement.

In the interior, the walls and ceilings are of white plaster and the floors are of granite.

Any additions or modifications should comply with this choice of materials.

The stone is carefully selected for many symbolic reasons, as explained, but the manner in which it was set also added to the symbolism.

Stone is laid in setting beds that are horizontal in varying size to emulate the sedimentary deposits of the Earth's crust.

Varying these stone courses is an important feature in the design where I used rough gullet stone to create an overall texture to the walls. The top and bottom of the horizontal sculptural walls and the openings around the windows or entrances all have smooth cut stone to crisply define all the edges.

Even laying the floor tiles carefully contributes to the geometry and the rhythms of the building. Sequentially shiny and raw textures parallel waves as reflected both in nature and the history of time itself.

The stones in the floor all follow the sinuous curves of the building, and they follow the exterior sinuous flow of the pavement outside. When replacing any pavement or interior floor, care must be taken to follow the sinuous curves of the design or it will result in a tragic discourse of the artistic expression.

Additional Architectural Elements
Any additional architectural elements should harmonize with the original design principles; otherwise they become "pimples" or thorns in the overall composition.

Handrails and Balconies
The handrails and balconies were all designed as continuous curves that flow around the building and down the waterfalls and pond in front of the Grand Hall to the river itself.

Ceilings and Added Paraphernalia
All technical paraphernalia should be hidden and carefully designed in harmonious recesses and alcoves, as originally intended in the design principles of the Museum. This not only minimizes the impact on the clean architectural expression, but leaves visitors free to enjoy the building without distractions and focus on the experience of the exhibits and artifacts themselves.

In the interior, the sinuous curves of the walls and particularly the ceilings are important elements in the design. Most of the walls will have displays but the ceiling is an important way to reinforce the sinuous unfolding of the architecture. That is why all the lightning, mechanical grills, speakers, alarms, etc. are hidden in coves.

Any elements tacked onto these dramatic shapes throughout the building are ugly distractions that do not respect the architectural intent.

Lighting
The use of natural light in museums was a novel idea at the time. A revolutionary concept for curators and interior designers, the innovations of the Museum are now seen as an inspiration for the design principles of world-class museums.

In the museum world, the use of natural light design to work with sensitive exhibits and control, as our team designed and recommended, is considered an asset.

Lighting is a key element in any building, but for a museum that needs to protect its artifacts from the light and other damaging environmental factors special consultants are needed. They designed a unique and original system of allowing indirect lighting to both accentuate the architecture and relieve harsh hot spots that would be unpleasant for the visitor's museum experience.

The indirect lighting in the coves accents the sinuous lines of the interior, and the indirect lighting lights up the architecture. Exposed lighting creates hotspots that would distract from the architectural form.

The Future
Any necessary spotlighting would have to be recessed into the architectural form so it would not clutter up the drama of the shapes. Such spots in the entrance and the Grand Hall and the colonnade in the Grand Hall thus have the spots designed in coves.

ORIENTATION AND FLOW

The flow and orientation is closely linked to its design and follows Cardinal's organic design principles. The orientation of the building was purposely conceived to open the francophone community to a celebratory enjoyment of the Ottawa River and allow a space to celebrate the diversity of cultures in Canada. The plaza was intended to gather the pedestrians into a meeting space where the Museum could host all kinds of celebrations, engaging the street and leading to the Museum's entrance, and further to the landscaped terrace of the river through the large staircase.

The Ottawa River
The river, the water — the symbol and source of all life — is the focal point of the Museum's design. This is not only because of its natural setting, but also because of the symbolic and emotional connection to the land and Canada's accomplishments.

Landscaping the exterior grounds around the river for people's enjoyment was paramount in my composition because there is no public building in Ottawa that fully embraces the Ottawa River like the Museum.

Even if the river bend is an old industrial site, the location offered an opportunity to wonderfully anchor Canada's culture in a beautiful and harmonious setting.

Particularly because of its site, the design was to fully address and embrace the Ottawa River.

The purpose was to engage the site as a park of wonders along the river itself. Hopefully, it would invigorate redevelopment in the national interest of old factory sites further along the river. The river could be the very bond to represent the various elements that combine the legacy of Canada in the 21st century, as an inspiration to all Canadians and international visitors.

The riverside entrances to the Museum flow outside with the river itself. Even from the Children's Museum, there is an outside ramp that connects to the outdoor children's playground so they can have a view and connection to the river.

The building mimics natural formations and appears as part of the land. Cardinal always understood that the buildings on the street might one day be taller; thus the roof and terraces were designed to be beautiful and useful areas to look at.

The rooftops and balconies are designed so all projections above the roof are sculptural forms that the public can use, not only for the views but for the enjoyment of the sculpture forms of the building itself.

All these roofs and balconies are designed to be able to be landscaped in the future as green roofs.

Provision for green roofs is addressing the future.

The plaza was key to anchoring the visitor, and unites the community in celebration. That openness and gathering space should be respected always.

The vision cones were an important aspect of the design. The open plazas allow the visitor to flow through the site and enjoy the magnificent Ottawa River and views.

Flow
Ultimately all forms in the building flow. There is no static point; the eyes can see what is next and invite the body to walk and discover it with ease and excitement.

There are no static forms or rectilinear forms that distract from the flow of forms and spaces.

Any composition should be part of the sinuous curves rather than a static composition that would take away from the dynamic flow of the building's forms.

All spaces are curves in action. There is not a moment that is dead or static. The design principles dictate keeping all lines directed to the flow. No patches of disconnected elements should be redesigned. The flow of spaces relates even between the different floors of the Museum's exhibits. The floors are not isolated or disconnected from each other.

In this way the spaces are not static, boring, easily defined elements.

The interior spaces are also designed to flow into each other so there is a continuous movement from one space to another, and through cross-referencing the spaces flow into each other through the four floors, including the mezzanine.

Yet there is an order and logic to the design of the Museum, since the Grand Hall is the central point and all galleries relate to it.

All the halls open up into the Grand Hall, so visitors can properly orient themselves.

No Black Boxes
A pioneer of its time, and still the largest museum in the world that showcases art and artifacts in natural light, the Museum eradicated the concept of black boxes championed by curators and designers elsewhere.

From my research and experience in travelling internationally on behalf of the Government of Canada, black boxes, although appealing to exhibit designers, were very disliked by the public.

Instead of black boxes in the exhibit halls, the ceilings are designed in sinuous curves 2 metres apart. In these curves there are slots and access panels so the lightning is delivered through the slots. This way the white plaster ceilings can be changed to any colour, texture or projected light effect that is desired.

Lighting has thus been very carefully studied to allow indirect natural light to be part of the exhibits. All exhibits have white plaster ceilings and walls not only to enhance the architecture, but offer new and exciting programming.

The designs of ceilings in world-class museums were important. We had special consultants from New York design these systems and ceilings who understand that black boxes fail to dramatically present the collections.

The ceilings and sculptured walls are designed so all kinds of lights and images can be projected throughout the Museum.

The Museum has 1,000 outlets for universal communication in fibre optics and copper, which can be used to broadcast internationally all programs developed in the Museum.

Visitor Experience
The unique organic curves and complex geometric composition allow a totally new experience for the visitor. The curvy aesthetics of the Museum are avant-garde and pioneer the new values of sustainable and organic construction in the 21st century. In this philosophy, the careful design elements make the visitor feel comfortable and excited, as well as a connectedness and belonging, missing in many other big cultural and institutional complexes.

Excitement and Adventure in the Flow
In this way, visitors are never in a static space that can be defined; they are always in spaces that continuously unfold. Their experience is such that they cannot truly pinpoint where they are because there is always something that moves into their field of vision. It entices them to continue to explore the whole complex in every interesting nook and cranny. It is like flowing down a river — every turn or bend in the river can open one up to new surprises and adventures.

Always Engaging
The cafeteria, unlike other museums where it is relegated to the basement or dark places, has a great view to relax, rejoice and reinvigorate before continuing to enjoy the diverse aspects of the Canadian experience.

Carrying the dining area to the outside balcony of the cafeteria relates to the landscaping area, to the lower plaza area and to the water pool in front of the Grand Hall. These public spaces permit the maximum light and allow the enjoyment of the outside environment as part of the Museum's program.

Reduce Museum Fatigue
The natural forms seem to fit the body itself, and the intellectual care of the Museum programming, and allow the mind to engage in a positive museum experience, therefore limiting museum fatigue physically and mentally.

It is important to not only have visitors appreciate the exhibits, but also have connections to the outside. This alleviates museum fatigue. Other designs are less considerate of the public.

People relate much more to dynamic forms that continuously appear as they move towards the space or as the light alters the appearance of the forms.

Care to Maintain the Flow
The unique design that harmonizes the human endeavours and natural environment keeps the visitor engaged, and is one of the reasons why the Museum is the most visited museum in Canada. The psychological factor of human nature always has to be considered.

SETTING AND MEANING

The design of the Museum is a carefully studied organic entity. As such, there is no doubt that, as with all forms in nature, the Museum will change and evolve its programming. Care should be taken to adapt these changes to respect the original design principles. The Museum appears as an organic entity rising from the land and as an elongation of our own human bodies. The architecture of the Museum is unique because Cardinal's design principles of balance and harmony clash with contemporary practices of architecture. While Cardinal's buildings aim to integrate the forms to nature, contemporary architecture harshly rejects nature and violently erects structures overpowering the land and forcing individuals to live, work and be entertained in boxes.

Provide a reasonable space between the Museum and any new development that may occur. Because the Museum relates to the forms of nature, closing it in might cause the loss of that experience.

In order to value the visitor's experience of understanding the Museum's mandate to harmonize and create a safe and nurturing environment to celebrate, refrain from overcrowding the spaces around the building and the inside.

The Museum is not only a symbol of a vision of a prime minister to celebrate the true wonders of Canadian diversity through its connection to the land, it is also the inspiration of values and harmonizing principles of what Canadian society needs to thrive in the 21st century.

CONCLUSION

The Canadian Museum of History is a cultural wonder that blends architecture and exhibits to display the unique civilization that is Canada. It is this sinuous blending that gives the visitor a sense of having visited a unique and special museum. It is a world-class museum that preserves and displays the most significant artifacts of Canada in thrilling exhibitions. The architecture itself is a cultural gem, the artistic expression of one of the best and, arguably, the most original architects in Canada. It is an artifact in itself, a masterpiece of modern architecture that manifested the vision of Prime Minister Pierre Trudeau to create an institution of Canada's own unique national identity. The Museum organically harmonizes the Canadian landscape with the cultural heritage, the architecture and artifacts created by all Canadians.

The architecture of the Museum represents the uniqueness of Canada as emigrant nations from all over the world meet, blend and learn to thrive with the Aboriginal inhabitants. The Museum not only unites the heritage of all Canadians through its artifacts and exhibits, but enshrines the brilliance of being a Canadian in the architecture itself. Douglas Cardinal is an example of the greatness that can exist when different cultures blend in love. A son of a German mother and a Blackfoot father, he personally embodies the Canadian value of multiculturalism. Cardinal was able to synthesize the different values of both cultures and expresses them in a single homogenous statement that is his personal architectural style: a signature style catalogued as classic organic by the experts of Kebyar.

Cardinal's vision of architecture is very personal, hence the need to understand the principles of his design. His Germanic roots offer a complex blend of western, advantaged technological advancements and rigorous discipline to comply with budgets and schedules. His French ancestry provides a love for the beautiful, the fine arts, the flare of form and the sublime. His Aboriginal ancestry gives him an uncompromised insight into intuitive design processes that blend the client's program requirements to the natural setting of the building. But the masterfulness of Cardinal's architecture does not merely come from his technological, intellectual or even emotional commitment to his client's vision. It is ultimately his spiritual commitment to a vision that is universal in character, and that ultimately creates a legacy that all who took part can be proud to hand down to their grandchildren.

The Museum is the epitome of such a personal and spiritual commitment, and the visitors feel the power and resolution of such a commitment in every cornice of the building. It is the most visited museum in Canada, and, while a visitor's feelings might vary about the particulars of the style of architecture, each one has an emotional response to it. The Museum represents a vision from a defining era when Canada committed capital funding to enshrine its great art, artifacts and material culture as testimony of its great nation-building efforts. The process was a feat in itself, a story worth telling to all Canadians about what it takes to create a wonder and a legacy for ages to come.

The Museum is a unique artistic expression of the art of architecture. Many awards, including the Gold Medals of Architecture in Canada and Russia, were dedicated to the Canadian Museum of History. A masterpiece of a single architect combining the design and technical solutions of dozens of architects and thousands of workers, the Museum is a monument to what Canada can do when all parties work together toward a common goal. Yes, the Museum will grow, change and evolve the character of its exhibits, but when the architecture itself is an artifact of such magnitude and relevance, those entrusted with it should honour and preserve its mission. Only a charter protecting the Museum as a heritage building will preserve the integrity of the vision and its mission.

The Canadian Museum of History is a place to rejoice, gather and celebrate. It is an institution that shows Canadians and the world the best Canada has to offer and, at the same time, bring to Canada world-class productions and exhibits. It is a place to honour and respect all cultures, and learn from each other to become more understanding of the human family. The future is bright for the Museum as the Canadian identity matures, blends with its history and acknowledges the Aboriginal Peoples' unique contribution. Indeed, the building itself represents the magnificence that can occur when all the cultures in Canada acknowledge each other and blend. That is the power of Canada, its legacy, its future to hold and share with the world — always.

LIST OF ILLUSTRATIONS

1. Douglas J. Cardinal portrait
2. Conceptual sketch, Douglas J. Cardinal
3. Inca stepped mountains, Peru
4. Stratification
5. Truss system, interior view during construction
6. Main entrance, exterior view
7. Exterior view of Grand Hall glazing
8. Rendering of Grand Hall with view across the Ottawa River on the left and entrance to exhibit halls on the right. Design architect: Douglas J. Cardinal, Rendering: Peter Schwartzman, Illustration Advisor: Philip Gabriel
9. CAD screen shot, Douglas J. Cardinal office
10. Computer model rendering, Douglas J. Cardinal office
11. Computer model rendering, Douglas J. Cardinal office
12. Formwork for concrete facade
13. Preparing for exterior cladding
14. Canadian Museum of History site, facing south from Place du Portage, May 2, 1984
15. Canadian Museum of History site, facing south from Place du Portage, April 29, 1985
16. *Goat's Horn with Red*, Georgia O'Keefe, 1945
17. Douglas Cardinal sketch of interconnections
18. Douglas Cardinal sketch
19. Riverside dome painting in the Grand Stair by Alex Janvier
20. View of Canadian Museum of History from across the Ottawa River
21. View of undulating Canadian Museum of History facade
22. Main entrance
23. Terraced plaza and pools with view of Parliament Hill across the Ottawa River
24. Main entrance with view of Parliament Hill on left side during winter months
25. Picture of the Spanish Steps
26. Canada Day fireworks at Canadian Museum of History over the Ottawa River
27. View of the Museum from near Nepean Point, model maker: Leonid Margulis
28. Rendering of the Laurier facade from the Maison du Citoyen. Design Architect: Douglas J. Cardinal, Rendering: Peter Schwartzman, Illustration Advisor: Philip Gabriel
29. Google Earth® view of Ottawa River
30. View of fireworks from Canadian Museum of History plaza
31. Conceptual landscaping plans showing circulation
32. Conceptual landscaping plans showing hard and soft landscaping
33. Plazas during construction
34. Plazas during construction
35. Plazas during construction
36. Cross-section showing the relationship of the exhibition halls
37. Section through the CINÉ+ movie theatre
38. Inside the CINÉ+ movie theatre
39. Main entrance oculus with Bill Reid's Haida whale sculpture
40. Interior shot from inside the Grand Hall showing view outside
41. Piece of Tyndall stone used in the Canadian Museum of History, showing a unique pattern